Why Can't You Afford a Home?

The Future of Capitalism series

Josh Ryan-Collins

—————

Why Can't You Afford a Home?

polity

First published in 2019 by Polity Press

Polity Press
65 Bridge Street
Cambridge CB2 1UR, UK

Polity Press
101 Station Landing
Suite 300
Medford, MA 02155, USA

ISBN-13: 978-1-5095-2325-2
ISBN-13: 978-1-5095-2326-9 (pb)

A catalogue record for this book is available from the British Library.

Library of Congress Cataloging-in-Publication Data

Names: Ryan-Collins, Josh, author.
Title: Why can't you afford a home? / Josh Ryan-Collins.
Other titles: Why cannot you afford a home?
Description: Medford, MA : Polity, 2018. | Series: The future of capitalism | Includes bibliographical references and index.
Identifiers: LCCN 2018019591 (print) | LCCN 2018020874 (ebook) | ISBN 9781509523290 (Epub) | ISBN 9781509523252 (hardback) | ISBN 9781509523269 (paperback)
Subjects: LCSH: Housing--Prices. | Housing--Finance. | Mortgage banks. | Banks and banking. | BISAC: POLITICAL SCIENCE / Public Policy / Economic Policy.
Classification: LCC HD7287 (ebook) | LCC HD7287 .R93 2018 (print) | DDC 333.33/8--dc23
LC record available at https://lccn.loc.gov/2018019591

Typeset in 11 on 15 Sabon by
Servis Filmsetting Ltd, Stockport, Cheshire
Printed and bound in the United Kingdom by Clays Ltd, Elcograph S.p.A.

For further information on Polity, visit our website:
politybooks.com

Contents

Figures

Figures

Figures

About the author

Josh Ryan-Collins is Head of Research at the Institute of Innovation and Public Purpose, University College London, a new research and policy centre focused on how the public sector can shape and create markets to deliver public value. He was previously Senior Economist at the New Economics Foundation (NEF), one of the UK's leading think tanks, where he worked for ten years and led a program of research focused on the role of money and land in the economy.

Josh has written two previous co-authored books: *Where Does Money Come From?* (2011, NEF), now used as a textbook in many universities; and *Rethinking the Economics of Housing and Land* (2017, Zed Books), which was included in the *Financial Times'* top 12 economics books of 2017. He holds a PhD in economics and finance from

About the author

the University of Southampton Business School and has published in academic journals including *Nature: Climate Change* and the *British Journal of Sociology*.

He lives in Brixton, South London with his partner and daughter.

Acknowledgements

The central idea for this book of a feedback cycle between finance and house prices was first published in the form of a blog – 'Fixing the Doom Loop' – I wrote in 2016 as part of a series of seminars on 'Rethinking Public Assets', co-organized by Oxford University Department of Politics and International Relations, the New Economics Foundation and Positive Money. The concept was further developed in the UK context in Chapter 5 of the book *Rethinking the Economics of Land* published by Zed books and co-authored with Toby Lloyd and Laurie Macfarlane.

I owe an intellectual debt to a number of experts – on banking, housing, economic rent and land and the links between them – with whom I have engaged over the past seven years. These include Richard Werner, Dirk Bezemer, Michael

Acknowledgements

Hudson, John Muellbauer, Claudio Borio, Tony Greenham, Michael Kumhof, Adair Turner, Alice Martin, Duncan McCann, Beth Stratford, Andrew Purves, Mariana Mazzucato and Steve Keen. George Owers at Polity Press and two anonymous reviewers provided valuable comments on early drafts of the book.

I would also like to thank Òscar Jordà, Moritz Schularick, Alan M. Taylor, Katharina Knoll and Thomas Steger whose path-breaking – and publicly available – long-run macroeconomic history dataset has been a key resource in tracing the historical relationship between house prices and bank credit and which I used for a number of the graphics in the book. The dataset is available online at: http://www.macrohistory.net/data/.

The arguments in *Why Can't You Afford a Home?* have benefitted from being presented at a number of seminars and lectures at the New Economics Foundation and the Institute for Innovation and Public Purpose, based in the Bartlett Faculty of the Built Environment at University College London.

And a final but large thank you to my partner Salome and our daughter Elsa, for their support and patience during the writing period.

1

Introduction

A remarkable transformation is occurring in advanced capitalist economies. Home ownership and housing more generally is becoming unaffordable for large swathes of citizens. In nearly all advanced economies since the early 2000s, the ratio of house prices to incomes has increased significantly above its long-term average (figure 1.1). The financial crisis of 2008–9 led to a fall in the ratio, but it has rebounded sharply since 2013.

Anglo-Saxon economies – where home ownership is deeply embedded in the culture – have been particularly badly affected. In big cities such as London, Manchester, Sydney, Melbourne, Auckland, Vancouver, Toronto, Los Angeles and San Francisco, median house prices have risen to over 7 times median incomes – with 3 times generally seen as 'affordable'.[1]

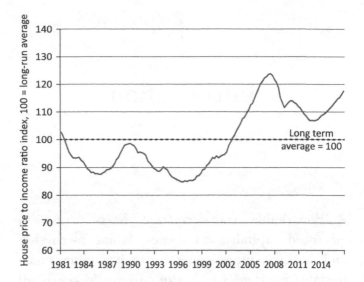

Figure 1.1. House price-to-income ratio indexed to long-term average in 15 advanced economies since 1981

Source: OECD Analytical house prices database.
Note: data for UK only available since 1987.

The hardest hit have been younger adults: the 'millennials'. In the UK, for example, in 1996 two-thirds of 25–35-year-olds on middle incomes owned a home; by 2016, this had fallen to just a quarter.[2] In the United States in 2004, almost 45% of the same age group were home owners, a figure that dropped to 35% by 2016.[3] In Australia, home ownership among the under forties declined from 36% in 2001 to 25% in 2015.[4]

The foundational promise of liberal capitalist economies that 'if you work hard enough you can have a home of your own' no longer holds true. There have been major falls in the levels of home ownership since the turn of the century across all the major English-speaking economies, as shown in figure 1.2.

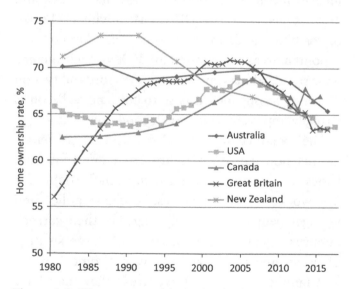

Figure 1.2. Home ownership in Anglo-Saxon economies since 1980 (share of all households)

Sources: US Census Bureau; English Household Survey; Australian Census Bureau; New Zealand Census; Statistics Canada.

Introduction

Rising house prices would be less of a problem if housing rents were more stable. But rents are also eating up an increasing share of household incomes. In the UK in the 1960s and 1970s, renters spent about 10% of their income on housing; by 2016 this had risen to 36%.[5] In the US cities where jobs are most easily found, there have been large increases in recent decades. In New York City and San Francisco, for example, rents increased from about a quarter of median incomes in 2000 to almost half (42% and 46% respectively) by 2016.[6] Meanwhile, 51% of renter households in the nation's nine largest metropolitan areas pay more than 30% of their income – the standard maximum ratio for affordability – on housing.[7] Saving for a deposit to buy a home becomes virtually impossible under such conditions.

The social, economic and political consequences of this housing affordability crisis are profound. Cities are becoming increasingly unaffordable for key workers such as nurses, teachers, police and younger people in the early stages of their careers. Suburban gentrification is rife with large swathes of urban areas cleansed of lower income workers and families forced to leave areas they may have occupied for decades, threatening the fabric of communities.

The rising cost of housing is creating new spatial

and demographic cleavages in society. Those lucky enough to have bought homes in the 1970s and 1980s in English-speaking countries have seen their net wealth (their total assets minus their debts) expand at a much faster rate than real wages. In the early 2000s in the UK, for example, house price growth was so great that 17% of working-age adults earned more from house price gains than from their jobs in many years.[8] In contrast, those born in the 1980s and 1990s have seen their wealth stagnating. They instead face a Hobson's choice of permanent renting in often insecure and low-quality housing or getting themselves into debt with huge mortgages many times their annual income, which require a lifetime to pay down. A study of Australia's two major cities in 2016 found that, in Sydney, 42% of average disposable income was swallowed up by monthly mortgage payments on a median-priced house in the capital, whilst for Melbourne the figure was 37.1%.[9] Increasingly, it is impossible to get on the housing ladder without a helping hand from the 'Bank of Mum and Dad', with worrying consequences for social mobility and equality of opportunity.

Recent historical research shows financial returns to property have outstripped other forms of financial investment, including equities, since the 1950s.[10]

Indeed, since the 1970s, wealth accumulation in many capitalist economies has largely been driven by increases in property prices via capital gains, rather than increases in profits from the production of goods and services. It is this dynamic that lies behind Thomas Piketty's[11] much quoted work on the wealth-to-income ratio rising rapidly in capitalist economies back to Victorian-era levels. This is a form of '*rentier*-capitalism', where life chances are determined not by hard work, innovation or entrepreneurial endeavour but simply by whether one is lucky enough to own a piece of land in the right part of the country.

These developments also have worrying implications for financial stability. Household debt-to-income ratios have risen to record historical levels in many advanced economies as people strain their budgets further to buy property. Such economies are more vulnerable to economic shocks and house prices falls, and central banks have less flexibility to adjust interest rates, in particular when mortgages are not fixed.

How did we get here? The explanation you will most likely hear in the media and from many politicians is that we are not building enough homes. The culprits are usually the planning system, the construction sector or excessive immigration. Whilst these are certainly relevant factors in many countries, they are not so useful in explaining the housing affordability crisis of the last few decades shown in figures 1.1 and 1.2. Planning systems did not suddenly become more restrictive at the turn of the century or construction firms more monopolistic. House prices have been rising even in cities with stable populations.

To understand today's housing crisis, we must go beyond just looking at the *supply* of housing and examine *demand*, in particular the demand for housing as a financial asset and land as a form of collateral. And looking at the demand for housing and the land underneath it leads us to consider much bigger questions about the social and economic structure of modern capitalist economies.

In particular, the increasing political preference for home ownership over other forms of tenure, coupled with wider shifts in political economy, have led to two important – and perhaps unintended – developments in the housing and land market. Firstly, the windfall gains that naturally accrue to landowners in a growing economy – generally referred to as 'land rents' – have been allowed to grow as taxes on property and the public provision of affordable housing have both withered. Secondly, and most significantly for explaining the rises in house prices in the last two decades, the deregulation of the financial system has created a positive feedback cycle between finance and house prices. Finance has become addicted to property just as citizens in many capitalist economies have come to expect to own a home. Underlying and perpetuating both these developments has been a failure of economic theory and policy to conceptualize the role of banks and land in the economy.

In this sense the housing crisis is about much more than just the housing market: it lies at the epicentre of the crisis of modern capitalism. To end it, radical structural reforms will be required to economic and public policy, including how we shape the market for land and regulate the financial system.

2

Land, Home Ownership and the Problem of Economic Rent

2.1 Land and economic rent

When we talk about 'house prices', what do we actually mean? We mean the physical structures that make up our homes but also what lies beneath: land. Land, as we shall see, has distinctive economic properties that mean that as economies develop it takes up an increasing share of the value of housing. A recent study of 14 advanced economies found that 81% of house price increases between 1950 and 2012 can be explained by rising land prices with the remainder attributable to increases in construction costs.[1] Figure 2.1 plots land prices, house prices and consumer price inflation in the US since 1975, indexed to the year 2000. It shows how changes in land prices have tended to lead house prices and are more volatile, rising and falling more

The Problem of Economic Rent

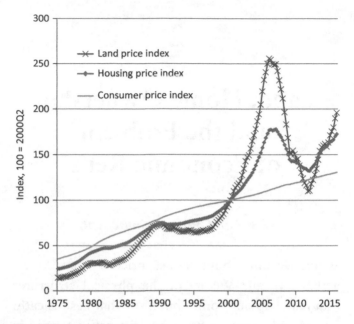

Figure 2.1. US land, housing and consumer price indices, 2000 = 100

Source: Lincoln Institute of Land Policy, http://www.lincolninst.edu/resources.[2]

steeply. To understand the housing affordability crisis, we need a better understanding of the economic dynamics of land.[3]

Landed property is land that has legal rights of ownership attributed to it. We take domestic landed property (housing) or commercial landed property (commercial real estate) for granted today, but these arrangements are not cast in stone. Throughout history, different legal arrangements over the use and exploitation of land have emerged. In modern capitalist systems and mainstream economics, however, the right to own land is taken largely for granted as a key plank of the modern economy.

The origins of this perspective can be traced to the British political philosopher John Locke[4] who developed a theory of 'natural' property rights. He argued that private property was antecedent to, and thus independent of, the state. Humans had a right to property when they invested it with their labour, as in doing so they removed it from the state of nature and improved it. Such activity was vital to create a civilized society freed from insecurity and the threat of absolutist monarchs.

As a result, private market exchange and private property rights are presented as 'natural' in mainstream economic thought, with their origins in universally accepted rules not subject to particular political or social arrangements. But the classical political economists that followed Locke rejected the 'natural law' argument. Adam Smith, usually recognized as the founder of liberal economic thought and *laissez-faire* capitalism, accepted the concept of natural rights but limited them to the notions of 'liberty and life'. In contrast, property was an *acquired* right that was dependent on the state and its form.

The classical economists recognized that land possessed several unique features differentiating it from other factors of production: capital (machinery, tools, computers) and labour (physical effort, knowledge, skills). In particular, land was inherently fixed, scarce and irreproducible – you cannot move it or make more of it.

The fixed supply of land for particular uses means it does not fit easily into standard economic theory, which assumes the supply of goods efficiently adjusts to demand via the pricing mechanism in free markets. To take a simple example, if the demand for mobile phones increases, mobile phone manufacturers can increase the quantity of phones produced – at a cost to themselves – until an equilibrium is reached, whereby demand meets supply and the market 'clears'. Companies could also simply increase the price of phones but, assuming a competitive market, they would face the risk that some consumers may choose to buy a different brand of phone. Market competition generates an efficient trade-off between quantity and price.

But the quantity of land cannot be increased in the way the quantity of mobile phones can.

If demand for land increases, the price goes up without triggering a supply response. All else being equal, this means any increase in the demand for land will only be reflected in an increase in its price, not its quantity.

As a result, whoever owns the land upon which this increased demand is placed is in a unique position economically. The ownership of such a scarce resource allows the owner to benefit from additional unearned income – what the classical economists called 'economic rent'. The landowner is able to capitalize on the price he charges for the use of land improvements made by other economic agents, for example the creation of improved transport, good schools or restaurants.

Economic rent from land can be extracted even if there are large quantities of 'empty' land that have not yet been brought into economic use, because more economically productive locations – such as city centres – are *relatively* scarce. As each location is more or less unique, control of every piece of land is essentially monopolistic, as Adam Smith recognized in his book *The Wealth of Nations*.[5] As a result, landowners can command disproportionate returns from those who must use their land.

The classical economists and later campaigners such as Henry George[6] were concerned that the ability to extract economic rent could endanger the development of the economy. As the economy grows, landowners can increase the rent they charge non-owners to absorb all the additional value that their tenants (such as workers, shopkeepers and industrialists) generate. Eventually, as rents rise, the proportion of profits available for productive capital investment and wages becomes so small as to lead to economic stagnation, inequality and rising unemployment. In other words, economic rent could 'crowd out' productive investment and incomes.

The classical economists' preferred policy to meet the challenge of economic rent was to tax it. This was more economically efficient than taxing labour or profits, both of which dampen productive activity. Instead, a regular tax on the increase in value of unimproved land – deriving from the investment of the wider economic community – encouraged landowners to ensure the most economically efficient use of their land. The state thus had a key market-shaping role to play in preventing the institution of private property from constraining economic development via rent. And indeed, taxation from property was a major source of revenues for US and European states in the eighteenth and nineteenth centuries. However, this view was not shared by the 'neoclassical' economists that came to the fore at the turn of the nineteenth century.

The neoclassical turn away from land

The neoclassical school believed that the economy was best understood as a self-equilibrating system governed by objective and universal rules shaped by market exchange. John Bates Clark, one of the leading American economists of the time in this school argued that Ricardo's 'law of rent' applied equally to capital and labour. It mattered little what the intrinsic properties of the factors of production were in the long run and it was better to consider them 'as business men conceive of it, abstractly, as a sum or fund of value in productive uses . . . the earnings of these funds constitute in each case a differential gain like the product of land'.[7]

Clark developed the notion of an all-encompassing 'fund' of 'pure capital' that is fungible across land, labour and capital goods. From this rather fuzzy concept developed 'marginal productivity' theory. Under this theory, land still has significance in the short run, when it is generally assumed that some factors may be fixed. For example, you cannot immediately build a new factory or develop a new product to respond to new demands or changes in technology. But in the long run – which is what counts when thinking about equilibrium conditions – all factors of production will be subject to the same variable marginal returns.

Early twentieth-century English and American economists adopted and developed Clark's theory into a comprehensive theory of the distribution of income and economic growth that eventually usurped the earlier classical political economy approaches. Clark's work became the basis for the seminal neoclassical 'two-factor' growth models of the 1930s developed by Roy Harrod and Bob Solow. Land – defined as locational space – is absent from such macroeconomic models.

Why land is different

In reality land and capital are fundamentally distinctive phenomena.[8] To refuse to see this is to guarantee that any subsequent theory will go wrong. Land is permanent, cannot be produced or reproduced, cannot be 'used up' and does not depreciate. None of these features apply to capital. Capital goods are produced by humans, can be easily replicated and depreciate over time due to physical wear and tear and innovations in technology (think of computers or mobile phones). In any set of national accounts, you will find a sizeable negative number detailing physical capital stock 'depreciation'.

The Problem of Economic Rent

The argument made by Clark and his followers was that by removing the complexities of changes over time (dynamics), the true or pure functioning of the economy will be more clearly revealed. As a result, microeconomic theory generally deals with relations of coexistence or 'comparative statics' (how are labour and capital combined in a single point in time to create outputs) rather than dynamic relations. This has led to a neglect of the continued creation and destruction of capital and the continued existence and non-depreciation of land.

Although land values change with – or some would say drive – economic and financial cycles, in the long run land value usually *appreciates* rather than depreciates like capital. This is inevitable when you think about it. As the population grows, the economy develops and the capital stock increases, but land remains fixed. The result is that land values (often termed 'ground rents') must rise unless there is some countervailing non-market intervention.

Indeed, there is a good argument that as economies mature, the demand for land relative to other consumer goods increases. Land is a 'positional good', the desire for which is related to one's position in society *vis-à-vis* others and thus not subject to diminishing marginal returns like other goods.

As technological developments drive down the costs of other consumption goods – cars, electronics, white goods – so competition over the most prized locational space rises and eats up a greater and greater share of people's income.

Housing and location is also different from other forms of capital because it serves two different functions. Housing is a consumption good that provides us with a flow of services (shelter, proximity to work and amenities, a place to raise a family). But housing is also a financial asset and store of value. Indeed, housing is by far the largest single asset held by citizens in advanced economies. These two functions can be complementary under certain circumstances. However, if house prices and land values rise beyond incomes, the financial asset function can come to dominate the demand for housing, which becomes speculative. This makes housing less available as a consumption good for large swathes of the population.

2.2 The rise and fall of home ownership

A home of your own. It's a common phrase and one with positive associations: a sense of comfort, belonging and security. Indeed, home ownership has increasingly become seen as an expectation, if not a right, in Western democracies, in particular Anglo-Saxon economies. And it is an expectation that governments came to embrace via important changes in public and taxation policy as well as in financial regulation.

But it was not always so. As shown in figure 2.2, it was only in the post-war period that the majority of citizens in English-speaking liberal market

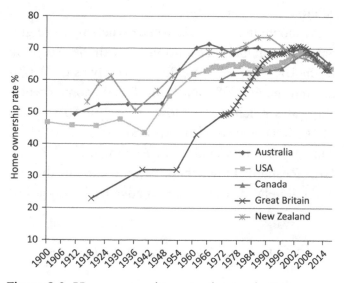

Figure 2.2. Home ownership rates for Anglo-Saxon countries (share of all households)

Sources: US Census Bureau; English Household Survey; Australian Census Bureau; Statistics New Zealand, Census; Statistics Canada.

economies came to own their homes. A major reason for this is that governments only began to prioritize widespread home ownership as a policy goal in this period.

In Western Europe, including the UK, where there was less freely available land than in the settler societies of the US, Canada and Australasia, it was not until the 1970s that home ownership became the dominant form of tenure. Today the average rate of home ownership across advanced economies is around 64%.[9]

As shown in figure 2.2, home ownership in Anglo-Saxon liberal market economies – with the exception of the UK – appears to plateau as early as the 1970s around the 60–70% mark. In the US, home ownership rates reached their lowest level in 50 years in 2016, having peaked at around 70% in 2004. A similar pattern is evident in Australia, the UK and New Zealand. How, then, can we explain the rise and fall in home ownership in advanced economies?

2.3 The post-World War II 'Golden Age'

After World War II, the state took on greater responsibility for housing in Western democracies as part of the wider reconstruction effort and a shift towards Keynesian economic policy. This involved the state using public spending, borrowing and taxation to manage demand in the economy so that high or full employment was maintained over time. Increasingly, the collective provision of basic social goods, including housing, was incorporated into this demand management process. Investment in housing was also part of a wider effort to build strong welfare states to counter the threat of communism.

In the US, a post-war construction boom helped create a thriving mortgage market. Generally known as a country with the least sympathy for big government, the US Federal government played a central role in the rapid expansion of home owner-ship shown in figure 2.2, mainly via its support for residential mortgage finance. The Federal National Mortgage Association (FNMA) – better known today as 'Fannie Mae' – was created during the New Deal reforms of the 1930s to purchase Federal government guaranteed loans from banks, allowing them to de-risk and expand their mortgage lending. By the 1950s, 40% of all mortgages were federally subsidized,[10] whilst a quarter of the increase in home ownership in the 1940–60 period in the US for younger cohorts could be explained by changes in mortgage terms driven by federal policy.[11]

Meanwhile, European states engaged in elaborate planning schemes in which housing, infrastructure, urban planning, and sometimes also employment and industrial policies together became an integrated part of a strong welfare state.[12] Specialist but conservative mortgage finance organizations – thrifts and building societies – were encouraged to expand their lending and given favourable tax treatment and conditions. However, mortgage finance remained largely within these 'specialized circuits', protected from the wider financial sector. In addition, home ownership was not (with the exception of the US) privileged as a form of tenure by state support: good quality rental and social (or public-) rental housing was expanded, and taxation systems do not favour particular tenures.

Both governments and mortgage lenders focused on the creation of large-scale, standardized urban developments, supported by the spread of cheaper and more efficient private and public transport networks, which also made land more abundant and thus kept land values down despite growth in incomes and populations.[13] These included company-, garden- and new-towns, European housing estates and American suburbs.

In many of these developments, land was either held publicly or cooperatively rather than privately.

This meant that the increases in the value of land from economic development – the economic rent – was captured collectively by the national or local state. The development of mass housing provision was an important part of the 'Fordist' growth regimes of the period. In the US the emergence of the suburb and home ownership created the demand for both automobiles and home consumer durables that joined up the circuit of production and consumption that drove demand.[14] Central banks and ministries of finance, who collaborated closely during this period, supported this regime by keeping interest rates on government and private debt low to encourage investment by both government and firms.

2.4 The collapse of Keynesianism and the neo-liberal turn

By the end of the 1960s, the decline in post-war economic expansion led to growing pressures on the Keynesian settlement. The collapse of the Bretton Woods regime of fixed exchange rates in 1971, followed shortly afterwards by the oil price and inflation shocks of the mid-1970s, proved to be the final straw. Lax fiscal and monetary policies were held responsible for 'stagflation': rising inflation accompanied by unemployment, as well as rising public deficits. By the late 1970s, monetarist and neoclassical economics re-emerged. The policy prescriptions emanating from these theories – collectively known as 'neo-liberalism' – emphasized the need to reduce government intervention and taxes and free up private markets, including the financial and real estate sectors, to increase the efficiency of the economy. At the same time, the demand for home ownership continued to rise.

In response to this, during the 1960s and 1970s, the Anglo-Saxon liberal market economies (US, UK, Australia) began to shift towards policies that favoured private ownership over other forms of tenure (rental or public housing). In the UK, for example, in 1963 'Schedule A' income tax, a tax on imputed rental income (the ground rent that a property owner would have had to pay if they had not been an owner) – was abolished. Five years later, when capital gains tax was introduced, an exemption was made for primary residencies. This immediately made private property a more attractive financial asset than shares and savings vehicles, both of which attracted hefty taxes.

In the US, the twentieth century saw the tax system become systemically biased in favour of land and real estate ownership over other forms of activity. Prior to the 1930s, property taxes accounted for around two-thirds of state and local government tax receipts. But gradually taxes have been shifted off property and on to incomes and consumers (via increasing sales taxes). Today, property taxes make up only 20% of state and local revenue.[15]

World War II saw the creation of a new model of withholding income tax at source, which made it far easier to collect by the Federal government and led to the centralization of fiscal power more generally.[16] States also began to switch away from property tax and on to sales and petrol taxes as the automobile industry took off. In contrast, property taxes remained primarily local and 'lumpy', requiring households to pay large sums of money rather than the funds being taken from their pay cheques. But even at the local level, property tax declined as a proportion of total local tax take and as a proportion of revenues between the 1950s and 1980s, as shown in figure 2.3.

Whilst prior to the 1970s property taxes were normally linked to the increase in the market value of the property (and hence land), whatever its usage or whoever the owner, in the 1970s a number of US states began to legislate to put limits on the

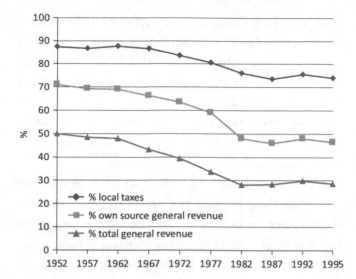

Figure 2.3. Decline in local property taxes in the US, 1952–1995 (% total)

Source: A.D. Sokolow, 'The changing property tax and state–local relations'. *Publius: The Journal of Federalism* 28 (1998): 165–87, 168.

allowable annual increase in property tax levies, usually either a fixed percentage or a variable limit such as the rate of inflation.[17]

Proposition 13, adopted by Californian voters in 1978, limited increases in the assessment of property until ownership changed. This led to further weakening in the previously uniform conditions of the property tax such as the introduction of classification exemptions relating to property usage or characteristics of the property owner.

The Problem of Economic Rent

The argument that there are differences in the economic value of different uses to which property can be put is certainly valid. But in practice, classification systems have tended to reflect the political power of property owners far more clearly than any economic differences: typically, farm and residential property is assessed at a lower rate than utilities.[18]

The maximum capital gains tax rate payable by individuals in the US between 1942 and 1995 averaged 27%, in contrast to 70% on income. Likewise for corporations, the maximum capital gains tax was 28% compared to 45% on corporate profits.[19] In addition, the tax code permitted investors to avoid paying tax on real estate at the point of sale if they reinvested their sales proceeds to buy new property of equal or greater cost.

Real estate is further favoured because land appreciation is not recognized in US accounting protocols. It is treated for tax purposes in the same way as depreciable capital – taxed income is considered to be cash flow less depreciation. But real estate does not provide a physical cash flow, but rather an imputed flow of income (or imputed rent). Property *appreciates* since increases in land values typically outpace the costs associated with depreciation of the physical structures on land. Yet real estate owners

27

typically are able to offset their tax against depreciation whilst capital gains are ignored.

These changes to taxation made home ownership increasingly attractive as a financial asset, as well as a consumption good providing shelter and security. In particular in the cities where rapid growth was occurring, home owners were now able to enjoy large capital gains – i.e. economic rent – from the simple virtue of owning property in an area of rising economic growth and investment. But there was no political constituency at the time to push back against these developments as the desire for home ownership increased and incomes continued to rise.

2.5 *From subsidizing supply to subsidizing demand*

By the early 1980s, neo-liberal policies had become more entrenched in the Anglo-Saxon economies, and governments began to withdraw from the direct provision of affordable housing and housing finance, instead enabling the market to take on a greater role. Private home ownership became the favoured form of tenure over renting or public housing. Rather than subsidizing or investing in the *supply of housing* or land – or indeed building or buying land themselves – Anglo-Saxon states began to shift towards subsidizing the *demand for home ownership*.

Selling publicly owned houses to tenants – often at a discount – became a popular strategy: it increased home ownership and won votes whilst at the same time reducing public expenditure, in particular the costs of maintenance. The most spectacular example was in Britain. A key part of Margaret Thatcher's vision of a free society was the promise of a 'home-owning democracy'.[20] The implication was that citizens could unshackle themselves from the heavy hand of the state by gaining a stake in society via property. In 1980, the Conservatives' 'Right-to-Buy' legislation saw 1.5 million publicly owned houses sold off in one of the most spectacular privatizations of public housing in history, worth £40 billion in its first 25 years.[21] The money earned from selling Britain's massive post-war national investment in housing was not given back to local councils to spend on more social housing, however. Three quarters of the cuts made in Thatcher's first period in office were from the housing budget. State housing provision collapsed and the private sector failed to pick up the demand, leading to a huge fall in new housing completions.

In other countries, policies have been subtler, but the direction of travel – towards the commodification of housing and privatization of land rents – has been the same.[22] In many countries, tenant protection and rent regulation laws were rescinded, leading to an increase in rents and evictions.[23] Municipalities were given increased responsibility for affordable housing provision, but saw their funding to provide it cut. As funding for maintenance was cut, the quality of the remaining public housing stock deteriorated and housing estates were increasingly stigmatized in the public and political imagination.

With cuts in the supply of affordable housing and land provision by the state, and the demand for home ownership remaining high as it became more attractive as a financial asset, house prices in Anglo-Saxon economies naturally began to rise. With large public deficits, pressure mounted on governments to find new sources of financing for citizens to be able to buy homes. The solution was to turn towards the banking sector. But in doing so, politicians created a new dynamic relationship between housing and finance, one which would come to dominate capitalist economies and ultimately drive up house prices even further.

3

The Housing–Finance Feedback Cycle and the Deregulation of Finance

3.1 Money creation, bank lending and house prices

When property prices rise faster than incomes, it becomes harder to buy a home. Mortgage loans bridge this gap, allowing households to access home ownership without having to save for many years. But there is a side effect. Banks *create new money* in the act of lending. When a bank makes a loan, it creates both an asset (the loan) and a liability upon itself in the form of a new deposit in the bank account of the borrower.[1] No money is borrowed from elsewhere in the economy. The main limit on bank money creation is the bank's own confidence that the loan will be repaid.

If mortgage lending supports the building of new homes, this new money can be absorbed into the

31

economy. However, in most cases mortgage finance enables people to buy existing property on existing land. As households, supported by banks, compete to purchase, the result is increasing land and house prices. Higher prices lead to more demand for mortgage credit, which further pumps up prices, and so on.

This feedback cycle runs against standard economic theory where an increase in the supply of goods, all else being equal, should eventually lead to a fall in prices. An 'equilibrium' price will be reached at the point when the quantity of goods supplied exactly matches the demand for them. But with bank credit and land, we have two phenomena that are quite unlike standard commodities. Bank credit is highly elastic and essentially infinite; in contrast, land, as discussed in the preceding chapter, is inherently inelastic due to its scarcity.

Figure 3.1 shows real house prices (adjusted for inflation) and mortgage credit as a proportion of GDP in advanced economies since 1870. Up until 1960, there was little change in house prices despite rising populations and incomes. Then, from the 1960s to the 1990s, house prices increased by around 65%, supported by the reduction in taxes on property and the withdrawal of state provision of affordable housing and gradual expansion of

The Housing–Finance Feedback Cycle

Figure 3.1. Mortgage credit and house prices across advanced economies since 1870

Sources: Ò. Jordà, M. Schularick and A.M. Taylor, 'Macrofinancial history and the new business cycle facts'. *NBER Macroeconomics Annual* 31 (2017): 213–63; K. Knoll, M. Schularick and T. Steger, 'No price like home: global house prices, 1870–2012'. *American Economic Review* 107 (2017): 331–53.

mortgage credit. But even more remarkable has been the change in the last 20 years, when real house prices have increased by 50%. During the same period, real average incomes have flatlined – but mortgage credit has risen exponentially. There is a clear correlation between the two variables since the 1990s.

The Housing–Finance Feedback Cycle

Causality – as opposed to correlation – is difficult to prove with regard to the effects of bank lending. This is because a bank's decision to lend is naturally affected by the demand for loans, which in itself is driven by what is occurring in the wider economy (most obviously rising incomes or increasing populations relative to the supply of new homes).

One way to test whether the supply of bank credit independently pushes up house prices is by finding natural experiments where the demand for housing is the same across a sample population, but some other, non-demand-related factor enables banks to increase lending. Regulation (or deregulation) can be viewed as such an example, as it is a political rather than an economic phenomenon. The evidence suggests that the Anglo-Saxon economies that deregulated their mortgage markets in the 1980s saw faster rises and more volatility in house prices than those economies that did not. But of course, a range of other factors could be at play, such as these economies also having less flexible planning systems and a less elastic supply of land.

It certainly appears to be the case that some Anglo-Saxon economies – the UK and Australia in particular – do have less flexible planning systems than, for example, continental Europe.[2] However, the legislative changes that impacted on planning in these countries mainly took place in the 1950s and

1960s, so planning rules are less useful in explaining the more recent explosion in house prices in the last two decades.

The visual evidence presented in figure 3.1, suggesting a close relationship between mortgage lending and house prices over the last 30 years, is backed up by statistical studies examining a range of supply- and demand-side factors. In a study of 19 countries between 1980 and 2005, the Organisation for Economic Cooperation and Development (OECD) estimates that financial deregulation enabling an expansion of mortgage credit has led to an increase in real house prices by 30%, far more than other variables.[3] A similar study by the International Monetary Fund (IMF) but extending to 2010 found that a 10% increase in household credit leads to a 6% increase in nominal average house prices.[4] The study also found that increases in house prices lead to a further growth in credit, confirming the positive feedback cycle between mortgage credit and house prices.

A further study in the US looked at the impact on house prices of bank branching deregulation, which benefited only certain types of banks (deposit-taking commercial banks) but not others (independent mortgage banks and thrifts and credit unions) in the same US states between 1994 and 2005.[5] It found that the increased funding enjoyed by the commercial banks from the deregulation led them to increase their mortgage lending by between one-half and two-thirds, which explained between one-third and one-half of the observed increase in house prices. However, the banks in the *same areas* that did not benefit from the deregulation did not increase their lending. This provides strong evidence that increases in bank credit drive up house prices independently of demand-side or wider economic factors.

Two circuits of bank credit

It is commonly assumed that the majority of bank lending flows to firms for investment – indeed, this is still how many economics textbooks describe bank lending. But today, banks in advanced economies lend significantly more to households for the purposes of buying existing housing and real estate than they do for either business investment or consumer purchases, as shown in figure 3.2.[6]

And there are good reasons for this development. Lending to a firm is a risky business with no guarantees that a loan will be repaid since businesses in most countries enjoy limited liability. This means that if their business folds, the bank has no legal power to claim back the value of its unpaid loan.

Figure 3.2. Mortgage credit and non-mortgage credit (commercial and domestic) outstanding in advanced economies, 1950–2013

Source: Ò. Jordà, M. Schularick and A.M. Taylor, 'Macrofinancial history and the new business cycle facts'. *NBER Macroeconomics Annual* 31 (2017): 213–63.

But when a bank makes a mortgage loan, it almost always demands the property as collateral in case the borrower defaults.

Figure 3.2 shows outstanding mortgage and non-mortgage credit (domestic and commercial) averaged across 17 advanced economies in the post-war period. Up until the 1990s, the two series move broadly together, but, as a proportion of GDP, banks lent more to firms and consumers for investment in production and consumption of goods and services than they did for domestic or commercial real estate purchase. But in the early 1990s, a dramatic change occurs. Mortgage lending in advanced economies increases from about 40% of GDP to 70% in the space of 20 years, whilst the stock of non-mortgage loans flattens, rising by little more than 5%. During the same period, average real house prices followed a similar path to mortgage credit, increasing by 50% (figure 3.1).[7]

This 'debt shift', as the Dutch economist Dirk Bezemer[8] has described it, is one of the most important developments in modern macroeconomic history. Credit lent to non-financial businesses – the traditional role of banks – supports capital investment and helps pay wages, leading to increased GDP transactions, economic growth and productivity, as shown in figure 3.3.[9] The increased growth in the economy enables firms to pay back both the principal and the interest, preventing the build-up of excessive debt overhangs.

But credit creation for the purchase of existing property and land increases house prices and debt

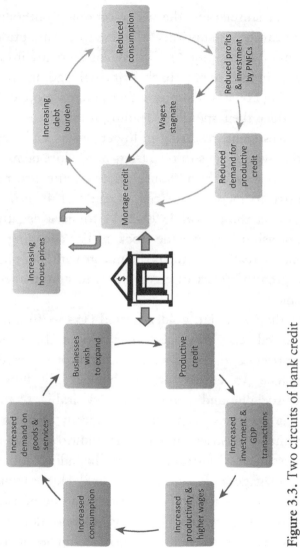

Figure 3.3. Two circuits of bank credit

without stimulating the wider economy (although there can be a temporary stimulus to consumption, discussed in chapter 4). This means there are insufficient funds to pay back principal and interest, meaning households must either take on more debt or reduce their spending, leading firms to cut back on investment, resulting in lower profits and stagnating wages. This in turn feeds in to more demand for mortgage debt as house prices continue to rise relative to incomes. Indeed, a study of 46 economies over the period 1990–2011 found a negative relationship between the stock of bank lending to domestic real estate and economic growth, but positive growth effects of credit flows to non-financial business.[10]

In the Keynesian golden period (1945–70), most advanced economy central banks and finance ministries used forms of credit control or 'credit guidance' to ensure private bank credit flowed into socially and economically desirable sectors of the economy, typically strategically important national industries and export industries, whilst repressing less desirable sectors, including domestic mortgage and consumer credit.[11] Home equity withdrawal, whereby consumption can be boosted via borrowing against the (rising) value of domestic property, was restricted in most countries in the post-war period.[12] Rising property prices thus did not feed in to rising consumption. Taken together, these measures insulated housing markets from the vicissitudes of financial speculation and reduced house price volatility.

But these restrictions on mortgage lending did not weigh down on economic growth because home ownership, although important in stimulating consumption and the construction sector, was not the key driver of growth during this period. Rising capital investment, including government and private investment and bank lending to firms (the latter particularly important in Europe) led to rising productivity and wages across Western democracies.[13] The combination of rising wages and low interest rates enabled households to buy homes and consumer durables on good terms with fixed interest rates, which in turn fed in to rising aggregate demand. Housing finance was thus part of a *virtuous circle* of demand and supply, but one driven largely by investment in the real economy rather than fixed assets.

How did Western economies allow their banking system to become so addicted to mortgage debt? It should be noted that the expansion in mortgage debt did not follow the same trajectory in all advanced economies. Different varieties of 'residential capitalism' emerged, reflecting the diversity of financial institutions, housing welfare regimes and political alignments in different countries.[14] But the emergence of this housing–finance feedback cycle was driven by the great home-owning democracies, the US and the UK, in the 1980s and the competition between the financial centres of New York and London. The financial innovations that emerged here eventually went global in the 1990s, as continental Europe was drawn in to the financialization of housing, leading eventually to the Great Financial Crisis of 2007–8.

3.2 Mortgage finance liberalization in the US

As described in chapter 2, the Federal government played a key role in supporting home ownership in the post-war period by offering to guarantee mortgage loans issued by private-sector lenders. However, the New Deal reforms of the 1930s counterbalanced this support for housing credit by limiting the ability of banks to expand lending when the economy was growing.[15] In particular, these reforms limited banks' ability to increase their 'funding' – that is retail deposits (see Box 1).

Box 1: How banks and building societies 'fund' mortgages

Banks must ensure their assets (the loans they make) match their liabilities (money they owe to customers) at all times. Since a bank's assets will be loans of varying maturities (e.g. a consumer loan of 6 months versus a mortgage loan that matures over 25 years), a bank's liabilities (what it owes to others) also need to have a matching variable maturity structure. In banking-speak, 'funding' refers to the matching liabilities a bank holds against its assets.

Deposits are seen as reasonably safe liabilities because, even though they are short term (anyone can withdraw their deposits at any time), in aggregate it is very unlikely that all of a bank's depositors will want to withdraw their money from a bank at the same time (a so-called 'run' on a bank) because governments generally insure a large quantity of household deposits.

Depending on the make-up of their assets, banks will hold deposits along with other types of liabilities, including savings products such as 2-year fixed rate bonds, covered bonds (backed by collateral such as property), or debt borrowed on financial markets of varying maturities.

As well as borrowing from depositors, banks also borrow on 'wholesale money markets'. The term 'money market' covers the vast network of deals involving the lending and borrowing of liquid assets in a range of currencies, generally between financial institutions such as banks, as well as non-financial companies and the government. 'Wholesale' means funds borrowed or lent by those financial institutions in large quantities, rather than the smaller amounts dealt in by private individuals. Short-term wholesale funding can be a riskier form of funding than deposits as the institutions that issue it are more sensitive to market movements.

Key reforms included the banning of interest on demand deposits, interest ceilings on time and savings deposits (Regulation 'Q') and the divorcing of commercial and investment banking (the

Glass–Steagall Act). As a result, mortgage lending was effectively restricted to more conservative savings and loans organizations – the Thrifts.

Innovations in the financial sector and the internationalization of capital flows that followed the breakdown of Bretton Woods weakened existing forms of regulation. From the mid-1970s, banks were able to begin to borrow funds from outside the US to fund their mortgages, in particular from the largely unregulated Eurodollar market. Domestic financial innovations enabled banks to get around Regulation Q and attract deposit funding away from the Thrifts.[16]

A new type of lender also emerged – independent 'mortgage banks' – whose business model was centred on the transaction fees that could be attained from issuing and selling on mortgage loans to the government – sponsored enterprises (GSEs) – Fannie Mae and Freddie Mac – rather than the traditional interest rate spread. Mortgage credit expanded rapidly in the 1980s to over 40% of GDP (figure 3.4). In 1975, close to 60% of non-farm residential mortgage debt was held by specialist saving institutions; by 1990, this had shrunk to just over 10%, whilst the government-backed and -subsidized GSEs had expanded to hold over 40%.[17]

Figure 3.4. US credit allocation by sector and real house prices, 1947–2013

Source: Federal Reserve Financial Accounts.
Note: Domestic mortgage data includes non-bank financial institutions' issuance and holdings of mortgage-backed securities by government-sponsored agencies.

3.3 Mortgage finance liberalization in the UK

For the majority of the twentieth century in the UK, mortgage lending was limited to building societies. These lenders operated a conservative business model whereby long-term property purchase loans could only be issued to those with a strong history of saving and mortgages were funded by safe retail deposits. Such arrangements maintained a link between property-related credit and the wider economy and limited rapid growth and volatility in mortgage credit and property prices. Quantitative credit controls applied by the Bank of England ensured banks lent mainly to non-financial firms.

But during the 1960s and 1970s, so-called 'secondary banks', including US banks, began to enter the London banking sector and lend heavily to commercial property companies, encouraged by rapidly rising land prices in the capital. In response to competition from these secondary banks and other financial institutions outside the Bank of England's regulatory remit, the 1971 Competition, Credit and Control Act brought a wide range of new financial institutions under the Bank's regulatory sphere (although not building societies). Importantly, the legislation also allowed the large UK clearing banks to borrow from the fast-growing wholesale markets sector just as the secondary banks were doing.

Margaret Thatcher's Conservative Party came to power in 1979 determined that the City of London would be in position to compete with New York. In response to the earlier deregulation of capital controls in the US, in 1979 the government lifted foreign exchange controls to open up the banking sector to greater foreign competition and give UK banks access to overseas funding, in particular the 'Eurodollar' markets. This meant these banks were no longer dependent on domestic deposits for their funding. As part of the 'Big Bang' financial reform of 1986, building societies were also permitted to borrow on wholesale markets and quantitative restrictions on mortgage lending for banks and mutuals were eased. No longer was credit to be centrally directed into productive sectors and repressed for the household sector. The result was an explosion in domestic mortgage credit from just over 20% of GDP in the late 1970s to 55% a decade later (figure 3.5). House prices doubled over the same period.

A key element of credit liberalization was to permit households to engage in 'home equity withdrawal', taking money out of the rising price of their homes to spend on consumer goods, cars or holidays. This led to the development of important new links between housing wealth and consumption and thus the wider economy. The expansion in mortgage debt in the 1980s was also supported by progressively lower interest rates (then controlled by the Treasury) and further subsidized by tax relief on mortgage interest.

Figure 3.5. Bank credit allocation by sector and real house prices in the UK, 1963–2015

Sources: Bank of England; ONS; K. Knoll, M. Schularick and T. Steger, 'No price like home: global house prices, 1870–2012'. *American Economic Review* 107 (2017): 331–53.

The 1980s housing bubble eventually burst in the crash of 1990 (figure 3.5) which left many borrowers trapped in 'negative equity' – around 20% at its peak[18] – where the value of their houses was below what they owed on their mortgage. This amplified and prolonged the recession of the following 3 years, which involved significant job losses, repossessions and a collapse in business lending. But rather than pursuing policies to try and dampen mortgage lending, the Conservative Party chose further financial deregulation, eventually contributing to Britain's involvement in the Great Financial Crisis (GFC).

3.4 *The rise of securitization and the globalization of housing finance*

From the mid-1980s onwards, mainstream banks entered the mortgage market in most advanced economies in significant numbers for the first time in the twentieth century, following the UK–US model. Non-bank lenders also entered the market often with the advantage of not having to fund large branch networks. As well as liberalization, a key development that made mortgage lending more attractive to banks was the emergence of a new financial innovation: residential mortgage-backed securities (RMBS).

In the standard textbook model of banking, banks hold loans to maturity and generate profits on the difference between the interest charged on those loans and the interest the bank pays to depositors: the 'interest-rate spread'. Securitization involves pooling together a range of different loans into a new financial instrument – a security – which can be sold to a third party. The idea is that by incorporating many different loans, the overall risk of default is diversified, making mortgage loans attractive to a wider range of investors, including large institutional investors such as pension funds or insurance companies who seek a long-term but relatively secure flow of income. Securitization offers banks an alternative source of funding (other than traditional deposits) and a different way of generating income. Rather than making money solely from interest, they make money on fees from selling securities backed by home loans. Securitization also enables banks to reduce their capital requirements since, in the pre-crisis period anyway, they could shift the loans off their balance sheets and into 'special-purpose vehicles' as well as selling them directly to investors.

The securitization of home loans had its origins in the US where the Federal government sought to reduce its budget deficit by selling government-issued and -backed mortgage loans from Fannie Mae to private capital markets. But there was only demand for a limited set of loans – essentially those with market interest rates and conventional terms. Subsidized loans with more favourable terms – those more suited to lower income earners – were less attractive. Securitization helped spread risk across the portfolio. Government-issued mortgage securities had a unique advantage over those issued by private firms: the government issues benefited from the backing of the state. These proved extremely attractive to US investors.

Europe and Australasia followed the American model – only without the government (officially at least) – standing behind the burgeoning mortgage market. This was made possible, in part, by the internationalization and harmonization of financial regulation along the lines of the Anglo-Saxon model following the collapse of fixed exchange rates and capital controls in 1971–3. Under the auspices of the Bank of International Settlements (BIS), which had been in operation mainly supporting transatlantic monetary coordination between advanced economies since the 1930s, a new framework was created – the 'Basel Accords' – that introduced minimum capital requirements for all banks related to the type of assets they held (including loans).

Loans secured by mortgages on residential properties only carried half the risk weight of loans to non-financial firms (50%) in the original Basel Accord. Furthermore, securitized mortgages, which were viewed as more liquid and thus even less risky, only carried a 20% risk weight. The effect of these reforms was to allow banks to earn fees and net interest margins on holding 2.5 times more credit risk in real estate than they had before without any increase in their capital requirements.[19]

Securitization transformed a geographically fixed and illiquid asset – a traditional 25-year fixed-rate mortgage loan – into a liquid and transparent financial asset which could be bought and sold almost anywhere in the world.[20] Opening up housing finance to a vast global investment sector broke down previous national and local institutional barriers over the funding of home purchase and transformed the banking system. Marxist economic geographers such as David Harvey[21] have theorized that it is an inherent feature of 'capital' to seek out new assets for commodification as profits from traditional forms of productive lending and investment begin to stagnate.

There is no doubt some truth to this argument. But innovations by the banking sector were also supported by favourable regulatory and, in particular, tax regimes themselves driven by the political pressure to provide widespread access to home ownership. In most countries today, there is no capital gains due on primary private residences. And most advanced economies also offer mortgage interest relief (MIR) on taxable income. In the Netherlands the foregone tax revenue from MIR was estimated to be around 2.14% of GDP in 2015 and 0.5% in the US.[22] Because the ownership of housing is skewed towards older and higher income households, this is highly regressive. Evidence from both the US[23] and Europe[24] demonstrates that it has mainly benefited higher income groups, many of whom will already be home owners.

Developments in Europe

In Europe, the liberalization and deregulation of finance was aided by the creation of the Single European Market and the shift towards the single currency. A number of pieces of legislation came into force in the 1990s to liberalize and homogenize capital markets and banking regulation. Banks across the EU were required to standardize capital requirements in 1993 following the Basel rulings described above. European integration also saw the driving down of interest rates. The 1993 Euro convergence criteria, introduced in the Maastricht Treaty of 1992, required member state governments to reduce their interest rates to no more than 2% higher than the three member states with the lowest inflation, pushing down European mortgage rates to historic lows.[25] Increased competition from non-specialized mortgage lenders – not least large banks – put further pressure on rates.

European mortgage markets doubled in size in nominal terms between 1990 and 2000. There was particularly explosive growth in Greece, Spain, Portugal, Ireland and the Netherlands, all of which experienced increases in outstanding mortgage loans of over 300% in nominal terms.[26] Many countries increased loan-to-value (LTV) rates from around 80% to closer to 100%,[27] making home ownership available to millions of people who previously did not have a sufficiently large deposit for a mortgage.

The combination of low and stable interest rates and the acceptance of higher levels of debt over longer durations by households and regulators in the 1990s made mortgages a more attractive form of asset for institutional investors such as pension funds and insurance companies who sought secure, long-dated assets. This coincided with the introduction of the Euro in 1999, which saw an explosion in capital market activity with the establishment of a Euro-denominated bond market. This was more stable than single-country bond markets and provided access to lower cost, long-term funding which helped develop wholesale market instruments as alternatives to retail deposits as a source of funding for banks. These included covered mortgage bonds – debt instruments secured by a cover pool of mortgages with the properties as collateral, but held on the books of the originating bank – and RMBS. As with the US model, banks would originate loans but then package them up into securities and shift them off their balance sheets either to special purpose vehicles (SPVs) sponsored by banks or directly to investors.

RMBS became an important source of funding in the UK, Australia and Ireland in the 1990s with some issuance in most European countries during the early 2000s.[28] Securitization enabled mortgage issuers to offer a wider range of mortgage products, to offer mortgages at much lower rates of interest and to offer them at higher LTV ratios. This in turn enabled larger numbers of people to access home ownership at higher price-to-income and mortgage debt-to-income ratios, the latter ratio increasing by a third or more in many countries between 1998 and 2009 (figure 3.6).

Not all countries engage in mortgage securitization – Germany, France and Italy are notable exceptions – but the trade in RMBS rapidly became a global market. Investors came from almost any country and included many conservative institutional investors such as pension funds and insurance companies. In other European countries, in particular Denmark and Germany, covered bond systems predominated.

The UK led the way in Europe in the securitiza-

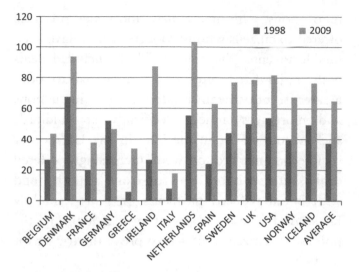

Figure 3.6. Domestic mortgage debt-to-GDP ratios in European countries and the US in 1998 and 2009

Source: European Mortgage Federation.

tion drive. Between 2000 and 2007, the funding of residential mortgages through UK outstanding RMBS and covered bonds grew from £13 billion to £257 billion, moving their share of funding from 2.5% of mortgage funding to 21.5%.[29] As a percentage of GDP, RMBS increased from 2% in 1999 to nearly 27% by the start of the crisis in 2007[30] and mainly explains the similarly sized increase in mortgage lending over the same period.

Liberalization and securitization led to financial

innovations with many new mortgage products offered to citizens who previously would have been unable to enter the market. These included deals with initial fixed rates which appeared to offer greater security against interest rate fluctuations and mortgages aimed specifically at landlords such as Buy-to-Let in the UK. In the US, poorer socio-economic groups were increasingly offered deals, often without any up-front deposits and with initial reduced payments or short-term low rates. And it was these 'sub-prime' loans to the poorest US citizens that was to prove the trigger for the GFC.

For neo-liberal governments concerned about rising budget deficits, encouraging the personal accumulation of assets such as housing equity as a means of meeting the cost of social care and retirement needs in an ageing population also made political sense. 'Asset-based welfare' began to emerge as a new policy framework with home ownership leading to less support for higher taxes to fund universal welfare provision and pensions.[31]

3.5 The housing–finance feedback cycle

The result is that in most advanced economies today, the housing–finance feedback cycle (figure 3.7) has taken a firm root. The combination of financial deregulation and innovation, increased expectation of future house price increases, greater opportunities

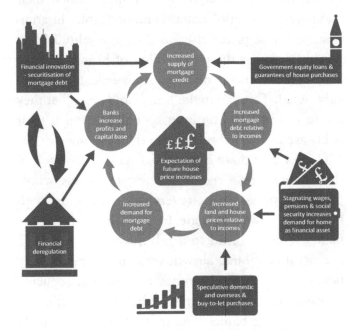

Figure 3.7. The housing–finance feedback cycle

Source: J. Ryan-Collins and A. Martin, *The Financialisation of UK Homes: The Housing Crisis, Land and the Banks* (London: New Economics Foundation, 2016).

for economic rent extraction via capital gains in land values, housing equity withdrawal, weakening real wages and welfare provision has proved a powerful mix.

The feedback cycle can continue for some time in a benign environment with low interest rates and secure wages. Such conditions allow households to maintain the repayments on their debts: their 'debt-servicing ratio' remains manageable. In addition, as house prices rise, so does households' 'net wealth' – that is the paper value of homes and the land beneath them, once mortgage debt has been subtracted. This can make households feel that they are in position to continue spending, even if their debts are increasing relative to their incomes.

However, if there is a serious economic shock to the economy or a rise in interest rates, the whole process can go into reverse. Households with larger loans will struggle to keep up with repayments. This will lead to a fall in consumption and a general economic slowdown. House prices may begin to fall if this becomes entrenched, reducing households' net worth and reducing the collateral value backing banks' mortgage loans. Eventually this can lead to a situation of negative equity and defaults. Bank lending, including to firms, will contract, leading to recession and, potentially, a financial crisis as the feedback cycle goes into reverse.

A situation can then arise where all sectors of the economy (apart from the government) seek to deleverage (reduce their debts). Households reduce their spending which reduces firms' profits leading them to pull back from investment and pay off their debts; meanwhile, banks contract their lending and rebuild their capital base. A range of studies show that such 'balance-sheet recessions' tend to last longer and be deeper than crises that do not involve credit bubbles (e.g. stock market bubbles); and within the universe of credit bubble-caused recessions, land-related credit bubbles are consistently deeper and last longer.[32]

Just as house prices can rise more quickly than rest of the economy, so they can fall, particularly where more speculative investors engage in fire-sales of property with distressed debt. This happened in the UK in the 1973–4 period and the early 1990s, in Japan in the early 1990s, and in many advanced economies after the financial crisis of 2007–8. The 'correction' was very large in all these cases, resulting in long-term economic damage to the wider economy. There is increasing evidence that modern economies are driven less by the traditional and quite short-term 'business cycle' that most economists have focused their attention on (typically a couple of years) and more by a longer-term 'credit' or 'financial' cycle (between 16 and 18 years) that is mainly driven by land and property values.[33]

3.6 *The Great Financial Crisis*

At the time, the Great Financial Crisis (GFC) of 2007–8 seemed to arrive from nowhere. Few economists or financial regulators saw it coming. Those that did were ignored or labelled as doom-mongers. The reason for this was that the preceding period, the decade and a half between the early 1990s and the crisis, appeared to be one of the most benign in economic history. The 'Great Moderation', as it was described, was characterized by steady economic growth, stable and low inflation and interest rates and rising employment in advanced economies. Central banks, most of them now operationally independent from governments, and finance ministers were celebrated as having finally found a way of ending the 'boom–bust' cycles of the previous decades.

The 'Great Moderation' was an illusion. Economists had been looking at the wrong indicators. The twin blind-spots of mainstream economic theory – bank credit and land – were interacting in a new way that was to prove economically incendiary. And whilst faulty theory may have blinded most economists and regulators, rising house prices and expanding mortgage credit proved politically too attractive to resist for politicians. It was a perfect storm.

The GFC had multiple causes, but the catalyst was the interaction between the financial system and housing in the United States. The US housing and land bubble had been building rapidly since the late 1990s (see figure 2.1). A key driver was the expansion of the type of mortgages that the GSEs were permitted and encouraged to buy. US politicians argued that these highly subsidized quasi-government bodies should be doing much more to help poor segments of the US population get onto the housing ladder. New legislation introduced in 1992 required the GSEs to begin purchasing mortgage loans with deposits of 5% or less for the first time.

The Clinton administration that took office the same year made home ownership for the poor a priority policy goal and saw financial 'creativity' as the key to the home ownership door. In 1993 new rules required that 30% of the GSEs lending should be dedicated to low- or moderate-income borrowers, a figure that was subsequently ratcheted up to 40% in 1996 and 50% in 2001. New asset ratios were also required for new categories of poor borrowers – 'underserved area lending' and 'special affordable (very low income) lending' – were also introduced. In the words of Raghuram Rajan,[34] one of the few economists to warn of the excessive build-up of mortgage debt pre-crisis, the US policy towards low-income households appeared to be to 'Let them eat credit.'

This led to increasing leverage and risk building up in the GSEs and the banks whose loans were being purchased by them; in particular, as the former had lobbied hard to maintain the favourable capital requirements and cheap funding arrangements they had enjoyed for the previous decades, despite the additional risks they were taking on. In 1990, only 1 in 200 mortgages had LTV ratios of 3% or less in the US. By 2007, this had risen to two in five.[35]

The US housing bubble finally burst in 2006 with rising mortgage defaults in the sub-prime markets beginning that summer but not peaking until the first quarter of 2010. This was not the first time the US had experienced a house price crash. But what made this one different was the fact that many of the sub-prime mortgages had been incorporated into complex RMBS and derivatives based on these securities (including collateralized debt obligations or CDOs) that were sold all across advanced economies, including to investment banks, pension funds, insurance companies and municipal governments. As the value of these assets plummeted, the market for these securities evaporated and banks who were heavily invested in these assets, including in Europe, began to experience a funding crisis.

There followed a sudden rise in the market rate of interest and banks stopped lending to each other, causing a liquidity shortage that threatened the payment system and entire financial sector. The authorities in the US, UK and Europe were forced to step in to rescue the banking system, lending billions in domestic currency to recapitalize banks. Only by flooding banks and the interbank market with central bank reserves on a massive scale via initial rounds of quantitative easing were central banks able to avert financial collapse.

The intervention of governments and central banks was large enough to prevent advanced economies diving into a depression. But the recession was considerably longer than all others that had followed financial crises. Government deficits ballooned due to the huge taxpayer-funded bailouts and long recessions. The housing–finance feedback cycle had gone global and wreaked havoc across advanced economies on a scale not seen since the Great Depression.

The European housing–finance crisis

The US sub-prime crisis that led to the GFC will no doubt go down as the archetypical example of a housing credit boom and bust, but it should not be forgotten that similar dynamics occurred in other Western economies, not least those in Europe. Housing–finance interactions are mediated by institutions, laws and cultures. Typically, boom–busts will affect cities – where the demand for land and thus prices are highest – more than towns. Cities also attract speculative foreign non-bank capital.

For example, in the UK, London and the South East have seen housing (and land) become the object of speculative investment by both domestic and foreign (non-bank) investors. The Buy-to-Let market in the UK has expanded hugely since the introduction of Buy-to-Let mortgages in 1996, whilst the annual amount of overseas investment in the UK housing market has risen from around £6 billion per year a decade ago to £32 billion by 2014, making up 17% of all foreign direct investment in the country.[36]

Restrictive planning laws in the UK meant that the mortgage boom of the 1990s and 2000s did not lead to a construction boom, which was of course beneficial in the aftermath of the crisis, as developers did not face enormous losses. In contrast, in the Eurozone countries – in particular Ireland and Spain – mortgage credit bubbles fed into construction booms with disastrous consequences for the real economy, as swathes of domestic and commercial property were left empty after the crash (figure 3.8).

Indeed, Spain and Ireland are good examples of why 'building more homes' can never be the simple

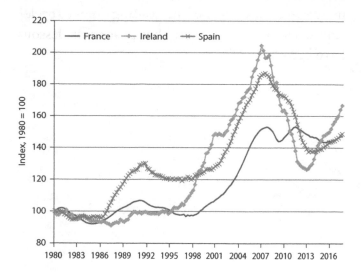

Figure 3.8. Real house prices, selected Eurozone countries, 1980–2016

Source: OECD Analytical house price index.

solution to high house prices. Irish house prices doubled in the space of a decade between 1997 and 2007, whilst Spanish prices shot up by 50% in just 6 years (figure 3.8), whilst both countries were undergoing huge construction booms. Prices continued upwards until 2007 when the crisis hit, defaults started and property values collapsed. However fast you can build, banks can create new credit faster.

How, then, did economists and financial regulators fail to foresee the GFC and, more fundamentally, understand the danger of the housing–finance cycle? And what evidence is there that post-crisis, lessons have been learned?

4

How and Why Economic Policy Went Astray

4.1 How rising house prices can keep the economy afloat

One reason regulators and policy makers didn't pay enough attention to increasing house prices and mortgage debt relative to incomes in the lead-up to the GFC was that economic growth was generally stable over the period. Financial liberalization meant that those lucky enough to enjoy rising house prices in the 1990s and 2000s were able to increase their consumption, at least for a period. This is significant because consumption makes up around two-thirds of national income in most advanced economies.

This house price–consumption effect works through two channels: a deposit channel and a home equity channel. Higher loan-to-value and loan-to-income ratios on mortgages meant that households needed to save less for a deposit on their homes, meaning they could increase their consumption in the present. Meanwhile, home equity withdrawal enabled households to monetize gains in previously illiquid housing wealth. Between 1989 and 2014, fourteen out of twenty European economies gained formal access to housing equity withdrawal.[1]

In particular in countries with more liberalized mortgage finance, there is clear evidence of a positive relationship between house prices and consumption.[2] Figure 4.1 shows the remarkable growth of home equity withdrawal in the United States in the 2000s running up to the financial crisis. Home equity lines of credit increased from 1% to over 4% of GDP over this period. There are similar dynamics in the UK and Australia. As a result, the stagnation in real wages and productivity experienced in many advanced economies in the 1990s and 2000s thus did not feed through to economic growth, which was being propped up by housing-financed consumption.

The build-up of mortgage debt also smoothed the business cycle by enabling consumption even when wages and productivity were stagnating. But it encouraged excessive leverage in both the banking

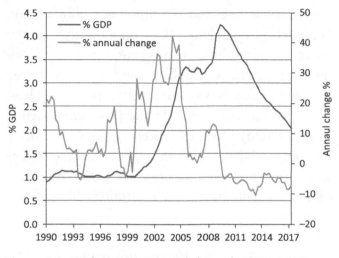

Figure 4.1. US home equity withdrawal, 1990–2017
Source: US Federal Reserve.

and household sectors that eventually resulted in fragilities that led to financial collapse.[3] The smoothing of the cycle enabled by mortgage lending was simply disguising the build-up of much larger, longer and more dangerous 'credit' or 'financial cycles' that macroeconomics had neglected for much of the post-war period.

Such developments fit well with the ideas of the late American economist Hyman Minsky,[4] who argued that 'stability is destabilizing' in capitalist, finance-driven markets. In the good times, economic agents, including banks, firms and households, become over-confident, taking on more risk as asset prices appear to be increasing continuously. To see this process clearly, regulators and economists need to be focused on flows of credit, asset prices (not least house prices), stocks of debt and financial as well as 'real economy' balance sheets generally. Indeed, economic models which incorporated these factors successfully predicted the crisis.[5] Standard neoclassical models that ignored such attributes did not.

4.2 Is housing wealth real?

Another reason economists and regulators did not worry about rising household credit levels was that housing wealth was also increasing and the rise in the value of this asset was seen to at least partially cancel out the increasing debt liability. In this view, it made financial sense for households to be able to extract some of this wealth to bring forward the consumption of pricier goods such as home refurbishments.

There are a number of problems with this argument. This first is that, even if we accept that housing wealth is 'real' or permanent, in the last 30 years advanced economy households have indebted

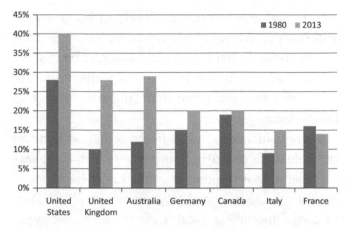

Figure 4.2. Ratio of total household mortgage debt to value of housing stock, 1980 and 2013

Sources: Ò. Jordà, M. Schularick and A.M. Taylor, 'The great mortgaging: housing finance, crises and business cycles'. *Economic Policy* 31 (2016): 107–52, 120; Reserve Bank of Australia.

themselves well beyond the respective increase in their housing wealth, as shown in figure 4.2. In the US, mortgage debt to housing value climbed from 28% in 1980 to over 40% in 2013, and in the UK from slightly more than 10% to 28% with similar increases in leverage in Australia.

Secondly, as the financial crisis made very clear, house prices are vulnerable to shocks, not least when they have been pumped up by rapid credit expansion, making it very hard to say what an equilibrium house price level might be upon which one could comfortably regulate levels of home equity withdrawal. More fundamentally, there is little reason to think that land values can ever be in some equilibrium, given that land is inherently scarce but economies that must use that land for production continuously grow.

Thirdly, increasing asset-based wealth as a means of stimulating consumption is a very inefficient way of generating economic growth. Large increases in net wealth are required to generate small increases in consumption via wealth effects or equity withdrawal. In addition, increases in wealth in housing are generally unequally distributed, tending to accrue to those in higher income brackets who are likely to spend less out of each additional unit of income they receive than non-property owners on lower incomes. Increasing the minimum wage or social security spending would be a far more efficient means of boosting consumption than pumping up house prices.

In addition, home equity withdrawal is rarely used to fund traditional forms of capital investment that will lead to improvements in productivity or innovation. Instead, funds are typically spent on home improvements or consumer durables. This form of 'privatized Keynesianism'[6] will thus have less of a multiplier effect through the economy

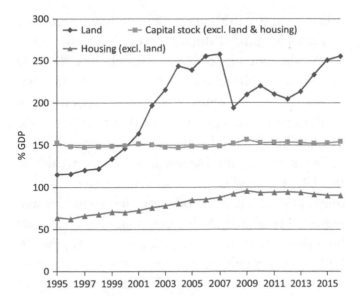

Figure 4.3. Non-financial assets as percentage of GDP in the UK, 1995–2017

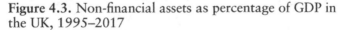

Source: ONS Blue book National Balance sheet 2017, table 9.2.

than traditional government capital investment on infrastructure.

Figure 4.3 shows non-financial asset wealth in the UK since 1995, including land, reproducible capital stock (including machinery, commercial structures, transport, information and communications technology, intellectual property) and housing structures. Capital stock is what the classical economists discussed in chapter 2 would have called 'real wealth'. They would have described increases in land values as economic rent. Since 1995, the volume of capital stock has flatlined at 150% of GDP, whilst the value of land has increased 250%. Housing (the buildings on top of land) has increased gently from about 60% to 90% of GDP and levelled out since the financial crisis. In other words, the biggest increases in wealth in the UK are flowing into something that itself is inherently scarce, irreproducible, unproductive and regressively distributed: land. Once you subtract land values from total non-financial wealth, the UK looks like a much poorer country – indeed, arguably Britain's 'real wealth' has been falling since the mid-1990s.[7]

4.3 The role of central banks

Central banks, in particular, must accept their share of the blame in failing to foresee the dangers of rapid mortgage debt and house price rises. In most advanced economies, they had been tracking data on lending to different sectors (including disaggregated data on mortgage credit) since at least the 1990s. But by the early 1990s monetary policy had become focused on a quite narrow objective: consumer price stability. The quantity of credit and money flowing to particular sectors of the economy and changes in asset prices, including housing, was of secondary importance. They key was to help the economy towards a 'natural rate' of interest where the trade-off between inflation and output would be optimized – the so-called 'non-accelerating inflation rate of unemployment' or 'NAIRU'.

This was best achieved, it was thought, via a public commitment to an inflation target (2% eventually became established as the desirable figure) and the granting of operational independence to central banks from governments in achieving this target. Under such an arrangement, short-term political pressures would not lead to excessively lax monetary policy at certain periods of the electoral cycle, which in itself could lock in inflation. But house prices and land values were not included in central banks' preferred measures of inflation, which instead were focused on the 'real economy' of goods and services.

The main policy tool to achieve the inflation target was adjustment to the short-term or 'policy' rate of interest. This is the rate that the central bank lends reserves to commercial banks. All commercial banks require such reserves to settle payments. The idea was that when interest rates were increased, commercial banks would pass on the cost of the increase to consumers and that this would reduce the demand for loans, which in turn contracts the money supply until inflation returns back to the target figure (and vice versa).

The economic downturns of the early 1990s and the dot-com bubble of the late 1990s led central banks, led by the Federal Reserve, to push down interest rates. But this occurred just as house prices and land values began rising rapidly in the bubble that would eventually lead to the GFC. Central banks also oversaw and sometimes initiated the deregulation and globalization of mortgage finance that took place in the 1980s, 1990s and 2000s, convinced that it would enhance the efficiency of markets.

In the mainstream economic theory that informs central bank policy, mortgage debt is theorized as a means for households to smooth their consumption and savings over the course of their lifetimes: the 'lifecycle hypothesis'. Rather than saving for many years before enjoying the benefits of home owner-ship, households are prepared to take out a large loan to increase their consumption beyond the level of their income at an early stage in their lifecycle in the expectation that they will increase their earnings in the future as they become more productive. As the household ages, its income increases relative to mortgage debt, enabling it to pay off its early life debts and also save for retirement.

If there is a temporary increase in house prices, this may have a 'wealth effect' and stimulate additional spending by home owners. But an increase in house prices will also see an increase in housing rents, which will mean non-home owners will need to save more for a deposit and thus reduce their consumption if they wish to buy a home. Changes to house prices are seen to affect the *distribution* of household sector wealth rather than the aggregate amount of household sector wealth and spending power.[8]

The empirical evidence casts doubt upon this thesis. For example, if the lifecycle hypothesis was accurate, we would expect economies with ageing populations – that is, most advanced economies – to see *lower* levels of household debt over time as a higher proportion of these populations would have accumulated assets compared to the past. In fact, the opposite has occurred. As discussed, household debt and mortgage debt in particular have increased massively in nearly all advanced economies as a percentage of GDP. In the US case, the bulk of US debt balances has shifted *towards* older households since 2003 and away from younger cohorts (with the exception of student debt).[9]

Evidence from the UK and Australia suggests that rather than spending their accumulated wealth in later life, households have been passing it on to their children as inheritance, whilst younger cohorts have increasingly been making use of mortgage equity withdrawal to fund large, one-off expenditures.[10] The lifecycle hypothesis also essentially ignores the role of home equity withdrawal which creates asymmetrical consumption effects. A rise in house prices will have a net positive effect on consumption in countries with high levels of home equity withdrawal because the increase in borrowing will more than offset any decrease in spending by non-home owners.[11]

The natural bias towards property lending

A further key assumption that informs the neoclassical notion of the 'natural rate of interest' that central banks use as their guiding light is that both borrowers and lenders have equally high levels of information about the risks they are undertaking when it comes to the loan. By choosing an interest rate that reflects this risk, the market can clear efficiently with the supply of credit meeting demand.

But in reality, a borrower always has more information about their future ability to repay a loan than a bank – in other words, information levels are imperfect and asymmetric between different parties to any loan.[12] Under such circumstances, it becomes difficult for the bank to estimate an interest rate that comfortably reflects the unknowable risk associated with the loan. An interest rate that covers this type of risk is likely to be very high and may lead to many reliable borrowers being priced out and only people with very high risk tolerance – 'gamblers' – choosing to take out loans. This problem is known as 'adverse selection' in the economics literature.

Instead of using interest rates to determine borrowing decisions, banks *ration* their lending quantitatively according to other criteria.[13] Usually, this is related to the borrower's circumstances. A common request is that the bank requires *collateral*: that is, a borrower's pledge of an asset to a lender to secure repayment of a loan. If the borrower fails, the bank covers its losses by repossessing the underlying asset the loan was raised against.

The most desirable form of collateral will be something that cannot be easily hidden or moved and will hold its value over time. Property – and in particular the land component of a property – fulfils exactly this criterion. The same properties that make land a desirable asset for investors make it attractive as collateral for a bank. A household that defaults on a mortgage loan can do very little to prevent a bank claiming their property.

In other words, all else being equal, there is a natural bias in bank lending towards collateralizeable assets, in particular home or commercial mortgages over and above productive business lending. This is perverse from a macroeconomic perspective because lending to firms for productive investment is key to economic growth, innovation and increases in productivity that enable wages to rise and debts to be serviced. It is this 'collateral channel' and the role that it plays in enabling increases in debt and consumption that appears much more significant in driving modern macroeconomic dynamics than any lifecycle 'wealth affects'.[14]

Some leading economists did recognize the existence of a collateral channel that could impact on bank lending and asset prices. Ben Bernanke, who became Chairman of the Federal Reserve just before the GFC in 2006, published a number of papers in the late 1990s that developed the concept of a 'financial accelerator', whereby rising asset prices could in turn generate increased credit and leverage beyond normal business cycle movements via collateral effects.[15] In such models, economic shocks are seen as being amplified via this channel, potentially over long periods. However, changes in credit are not seen as *independently* causing shocks or major changes to output or inflation.

Presumably because of this, the financial accelerator theory – which came to be closely followed by central banks – did not advocate intervention by regulators to try and dampen credit cycles. The consensus was that it was better to wait for the bust and 'clean up afterwards' than attempt to contain/prevent the boom altogether.[16] First, it was thought difficult to ascertain when asset prices had risen 'beyond fundamentals' and there was a danger that by intervening too early, an unnecessary squeeze might be placed on credit-fuelled expansion. Secondly, monetary policy approaches had become limited to the use of short-term interest rates, rather than adjustments to credit quantities and this was felt to be too blunt a tool to target a narrow part of the market such as property prices. And more generally, it was felt that rising house prices were a sign of – and could support – healthy economic growth.

But recent research shows that increases in land and house prices may have a 'crowding out' effect on bank lending to non-financial firms in favour of mortgage lending. A study of bank lending in the US found that increases in house prices led banks to substitute away from commercial lending towards mortgage lending.[17] The authors found that this resulted in a decrease in the investments of firms that had a relationship with the affected banks. In other words, increasing land prices negatively and potentially permanently affected business investment via reduced lending.

4.4 The post-crisis feedback cycle

Have the lessons of the GFC been learned? Post-crisis, while maintaining consumer price inflation as their primary target, central banks have begun to take a closer interest in monitoring house prices and introduced policies aimed at restricting real estate credit to address 'systemic risks' across national economies – so-called 'macroprudential' policies.[18] Regulators have imposed limits to loan-to-value and loan-to-income ratios for mortgages and also targeted Buy-to-Let and interest-only mortgages in the UK, Australia, Switzerland, New Zealand and Hong Kong.

Such policies are welcome but there is little sign as yet they are sufficient to overcome the strong incentives banks have to lend against landed property. After previous house price bubbles, the house price-to-income ratio has generally returned to somewhere near its long-term average. Not so this time. Despite the new regulations in many advanced economies, there is every sign of mortgage expansion and house price growth at rates well above GDP growth and incomes.

Some of the richest and most sophisticated economies in the world now seem to have become caught up in another mortgage credit/house price bubble. House prices in Toronto, Canada, have doubled in the last 5 years. Total outstanding US mortgage loans are now back at nearly $15 trillion, the same as at the 2008 crisis peak. In Sweden, the household debt-to-income ratio reached 179% in 2015, a higher rate than the crisis peak in the US in 2008.[19] A similar story applies in the Netherlands, Norway and Belgium. Meanwhile, Australia and New Zealand are the champions of the post-crisis house price boom, seeing the value of property increase from three to four times GDP in the space of just 4 years since 2012,[20] racing far ahead of incomes. The two largest cities, Sydney and Melbourne, averaged 14% and 10% annual increases in house prices between 2013 and 2017 respectively. And whilst average house prices did fall markedly in the UK and US, real wages have also flatlined, meaning affordability has not increased as rapidly as might have been expected.

A wall of liquidity

Despite taking some steps to regulate mortgage credit, governments and central banks must both shoulder the blame for the emergence of this latest house-price boom. Post-crisis, Western governments, in particular the US, embarked on an initial Keynesian-type fiscal stimulus, which helped prevent a depression and for a while looked to have revived economic growth. But once things appeared to be improving growth-wise, governments became obsessed with reducing the large public deficits that had naturally built up following the bank bailouts and recessions that followed the crisis. Governments cut back on spending and hoped that easy monetary policy – low interest rates – would encourage consumption and investment. The market, it was hoped, would come back to life now that the recovery was seemingly under way.

Interest rates were reduced to and held at zero in nearly all advanced economies in the post-crisis period, but there was little sign of a recovery. Economists argued that the crisis had given rise to special conditions whereby even very low interest rate loans were not attractive to confidence-sapped businesses. As a result, central banks embarked on a new policy: quantitative easing (QE). Since 2009, the US, UK, Japanese and European central banks have together bought up more than $11 trillon-worth (as of early 2018) of government bonds and other safe assets from investors, replacing it with zero-interest newly created money. The hope was that this would force investors to invest in more risky, real economy debt such as debt and equity issued by companies.

This huge monetary expansion had remarkably little effect on economic growth and business investment in advanced economies, which in many cases are only just returning to the levels enjoyed pre-crisis. But what QE has done is pump up asset prices, in particular house prices. The 'wall of liquidity' created by QE catalysed a global search for higher yielding but safe assets. Landed property, particularly in international cities, proved to be one of the most attractive assets for investors with global reach, not least because they could easily source borrowing, backed by property assets, at ultra-low interest rates from a banking sector still hooked on real estate.

With real interest rates on many government bonds at zero or even negative in the last few years, real estate in 'global cities' such as Paris, New York, London, Hong Kong and Toronto has become akin to gold – an essentially speculative but still 'safe' store of value. Property prices in these cities have 'synchronized', with price dynamics closer to each other than with domestic cities and regions.[21] Although speculative buyers from both home and abroad usually target 'prime' (very expensive) properties, this naturally raises prices across these cities and means they become unaffordable for those on middle incomes. In London, for example, a recent study found that an increase of 1 percentage point in the volume share of residential transactions registered to overseas companies led to an increase of about 2.1% in house prices.[22] The Mayor of London has ordered a study on foreign ownership in the capital after property prices rose by 54% in 4 years.

In the US, where house prices have overtaken the nominal level they reached at the height of the crisis, the National Association of Realtors estimates that Chinese investors bought 29,000 American homes for a total of $27 billion in the year to March 2016.[23] Foreign buyers focus on a handful of cities: San Francisco, Seattle, New York and Miami. In the latter, apartments are being built in numbers not seen since the financial crisis, financed in part by Venezuelan money. In Australia, Sydney and Melbourne have also been the target of huge investments by Asian investors.

The private and social housing sectors in advanced economies have also been affected, being increasingly financialized over the years since the crisis. The private rented sector has been opened to foreign investment, with private equity funds, hedge funds, sovereign wealth funds, Real Estate Investment Trusts and other types of financial/real estate investors buying up property at low prices and ramping up rents. Affordable housing projects that were previously state-funded have been opened up into private rental markets, driving up social rents.[24] Reduced state funding has led to housing associations adopting much more profit-oriented strategies.[25]

Securitization redux

Perhaps the most remarkable development in the finance-housing feedback cycle story since the financial crisis has been the re-embracing of securitization – the financial innovation seen as the key cause of excessive housing bubbles and financial instability – by advanced economies. RMBS markets collapsed after the crisis and regulators took a number of steps to make securitization transactions safer and ensure that appropriate incentives were put in place to manage risk. This included higher capital requirements and mandatory risk retention for the originator bank to ensure they kept some 'skin in the game', challenging the 'originate and distribute' model described in the previous chapter.

However, regulators and central banks have also played a key role in saving securitization markets from oblivion. In the US, the recovery in RMBS has mainly been thanks to the actions of the Federal Reserve which rescued the GSE – Fannie Mae and Freddie Mac – by taking billions of dollars' worth of RMBS onto its balance sheet, enabling them to gradually return to financial health. Currently these agencies guarantee around 80% of all US mortgage debt in the US's 'socialized' mortgage market. Private label RMBS have fared noticeably less well. Meanwhile, the European Central Bank (ECB) has single-handedly kept the European securitization market alive by offering commercial banks a vast flow of cheap loans in return for a wide range of asset-backed securities, including RMBS as collateral.[26]

Indeed, European central banks have argued that it is vital to revitalize the European asset-backed securities market for the health of the wider European economy.[27] The ECB and the European Commission have identified the development of a 'simple', 'transparent' and 'standardized' (STS) securitization market as a key building block of its Capital Markets Union (CMU), a collection of EU initiatives aimed at developing non-bank lending and capital market financing. In policy announcements, the European Commission has focused on this a means of catalysing infrastructure and financing for small and medium-sized enterprises (SMEs), both of which are seen as priorities for jobs and growth. But in reality there are very few examples of successful SME and infrastructure funding via securitization. The risks attached to these loans tend to be too idiosyncratic to be bundled together. In contrast, real estate-backed securities have always been much easier to securitize. Under the proposed legislation, securitizations that meet certain criteria will be eligible for STS classification, which will allow for softer prudential treatment via lower capital charges.

One of the key justifications for STS is that the problems caused by securitization in the financial crisis were mainly concentrated in the US and that European markets were much more resilient. But there are important legal differences relating to mortgage loans between the US and the EU. In the EU, all mortgage loans are 'full recourse' loans. This means that, following a default, the lender can foreclose the secured asset and also has recourse to the borrower, meaning that the lender can also collect the debt from the borrower's unsecured personal assets and their future income. This difference has a crucial impact on the incentives facing borrowers who are struggling to make repayments. Indeed, the US states which did not have full recourse laws had 30% lower rates of default than those that did.[28] In other words, the 'safety' of securitization practices is likely to have much more to do with bankruptcy laws than anything to do with differences between Europe and the US.

Surprisingly, there are no thresholds for loan-to-value or loan-to-income ratios for mortgages to be eligible for STS securitizations, even though these are the most important indicators for risk in mortgage lending. So legal protection from predatory lending or the prevention of unsustainable investment likely leading to house price bubbles is not the aim of the new STS label. In addition, the legal documents describing STS encourage the use of derivatives such as exchange-rate and interest-rate swaps in the creation of securities even though, again, these were widely seen as a key cause of the crisis.[29]

A more persuasive explanation for the STS programme is that it is designed primarily to support Europe's very large mortgage lenders. Many of these banks, particularly in the UK and the Netherlands, still hold large quantities of securitized assets on their balance sheets from the pre-crisis period. Many of them are coming to maturity and will need rolling over in the coming years.[30] It is vital that the banks have a source of funding for these loans to prevent another crunch in liquidity. It would appear that rather than addressing the root cause of the financial crisis of 2007–8 in the misallocation of credit to the housing market, in part enabled by securitization, European authorities have instead focused on how to prop up a bloated and real-estate addicted banking sector by repositioning securitization as an attractive and safe form of investment attracting lower capital requirements.

In summary, in their efforts to kick-start the economy and revive the banking system post-crisis, governments and central banks have drawn capital markets and a range of other global investors into the housing–finance feedback cycle. Real estate, in particular in the world's global cities, has become the preferred store of value in the face of collapsing yields on government bonds. This wall of liquidity has been good for the banking system, which itself remains largely orientated towards property-backed loans over other types of lending. It has not been good news for the citizens of advanced economies who have seen their wages fail to keep pace with rising land and property prices.

5

Breaking
the Housing–Finance
Feedback Cycle

5.1 Introduction

Today, governments are becoming seriously concerned about housing affordability. However, the identification of the cause of rising house prices focuses on the supply side, reflecting mainstream economic theory and its neglect of the unique and contrasting properties of land and credit. Politicians of both Left and Right of the political spectrum are guilty of this. Typically, progressives advocate building more homes with little consideration of the fact that desirable location (typically in large cities) is inherently limited. Meanwhile, free-market liberals and economists claim that all will be solved if planning rules can be liberalized, neglecting the fact that planning rules are themselves an outcome of land's scarcity and people's almost limitless desire to live in attractive places.

This is not to say that sensible changes to planning laws or more investment in good quality, affordable housing in the right places would make no difference to house prices. But the fundamental driver of high house prices in advanced economies comes from excessive speculative demand, not a lack of supply.

To recap, housing can serve two economic functions. It is both a consumption good, providing us with shelter, proximity to work, a place to raise a family. But equally and increasingly it serves another function: a financial asset. A financial asset that can provide increases in paper wealth far in excess of other forms of asset such as savings, shares and, in particular, government bonds. This has been particularly noticeable in the last decades, but in fact property has been the best form of investment going back 130 years in advanced economies, averaging the same 7% annual return as equities but being far less volatile.[1] And importantly, in Anglo-Saxon liberal market economies, home ownership has enabled households to borrow against the rising value of their property, propping up consumption as wages have stagnated.

This wider role of housing and land as a means of boosting consumption is one reason that politicians have been reluctant to address demand-side issues and the housing–finance feedback cycle. Added to this is the problem that the banking sector's health has become increasingly intertwined with house prices as mortgage debt has become the key asset on their balance sheets. Falling house prices will lead to falling collateral values relative to outstanding debts, leading banks to contract even further their lending to businesses. And, finally, there is the simple political fact that the majority of the voting population in advanced economies are themselves home owners. And their homes make up by far their largest source of wealth.

Despite this gloomy prognosis, there are reasons to be hopeful. Falling home ownership is creating a new constituency of voters demanding a better deal from governments, in particular amongst younger swathes of the population. London, for example, has just recently became a majority renting city. And, although the general pattern of increasing mortgage debt and house prices is common across many advanced economies, there are some important exceptions. Economically successful advanced economies such as Germany, Austria, Japan, South Korea and Singapore have actually seen average house prices falling relative to incomes since the 1990s, as shown in figure 5.1.

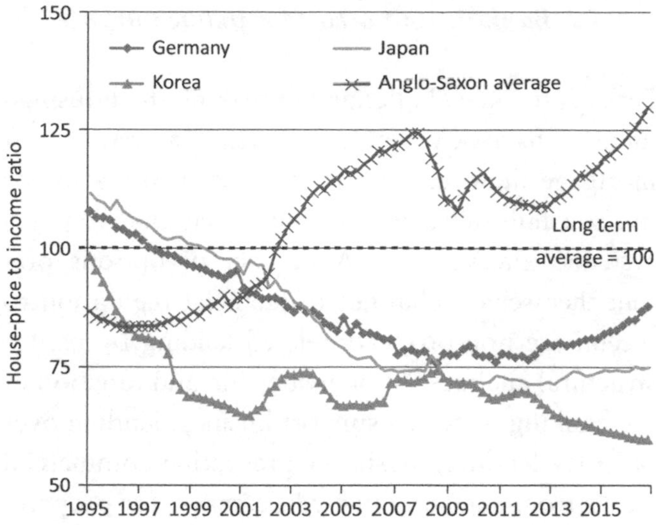

Figure 5.1. House price-to-income ratios in Germany, Japan, Korea and Anglo-Saxon economies indexed to long-term average (100), 1995–2016

Source: OECD Analytical house price database.

These economies share some similar characteristics, in particular in the way they govern the land market, tenure policies and their respective banking systems. This chapter draws on these cases to examine how we might break the housing–finance cycle by looking at three main areas of reform: financial reform, tax reform and changes to the usage and ownership of land.

97

5.2 Banking and credit for public purpose

Perhaps the key challenge in breaking the housing–finance feedback cycle is weaning banks off mortgage finance. This is more than just a minor 'market failure'; it is a systemic bias that requires systemic intervention. A number of options present themselves: changes to financial regulation to incentivize non-property-related lending by banks; structural changes to the ownership and function of the banking sector to support business lending over property lending; or simply preventing commercial banks from engaging in credit creation for property purchase and turning to other forms of property financing.

Rather than focusing purely on the price of credit (interest rates), policy makers should consider regulating the quantity and allocation of credit for different purposes. During their history, almost all central banks have employed forms of formal and informal quantity-based credit regulation under various terms including 'credit controls', 'the direction of credit', 'credit guidance', 'the framing of credit', 'window guidance' or 'moral suasion'.[2]

Credit controls were particular effective in East Asian economies. They were adopted by the Japanese, Korean and Taiwanese central banks in the early 1940s during World War II and in the decades that followed.[3] Called 'window guidance' in these countries, the central bank determined a desired rate of nominal GDP growth, calculated the necessary amount of credit to achieve this and then allocated this lending across both various types of banks – many of which were publicly owned – and industrial sectors.

Credit for the purchase of land and property was suppressed under these regimes as it was seen to produce excessive asset price inflation and subsequent banking crises. Most bank credit was allocated to productive use, either investment in plant and equipment to produce more goods, investment to offer more services, or other forms of investment that enhanced productivity (such as the implementation of new technologies, processes, and know-how) – and often a combination of these.[4] East Asia famously enjoyed one of the fastest periods of sustained economic growth during the period when these credit controls were in place. There were no major credit bubbles in the housing sector.

Domestic regulations of this type would be considerably more effective if they were complemented by supportive international regulation. International regulators, including the BIS and the IMF, need to reverse the strong favouritism shown towards property lending in terms of capital and liquidity requirements for the banking sector. Regulations should support banks that are able to de-risk their loans via methods other than land-based collateral, most obviously via the building up of long-term relationships with non-financial businesses, as discussed in the next section. And finally, there is a strong case that all but the simplest forms of asset-backed securitization should be prohibited.

Structural reforms to the banking sector

There may be limits to what regulation can achieve on its own given how entrenched mortgage assets have become on modern banks' balance sheets. In addition, the highly competitive and globalized nature of banking and capital flows today makes regulation easier to 'game'. Countries might have to re-impose foreign exchange and capital controls to prevent foreign banks and shadow banking structures from getting around domestic rules. Structural reforms may then be more effective.

A range of studies suggests that bank-lending behaviour is strongly influenced by ownership type, size and other institutional factors. Since the 1990s, advanced economy banking systems have become less diverse as financial deregulation led to waves of mergers and acquisitions, not least following financial crises. Large, universal shareholder banks that combine investment and retail banking functions have become the dominant model in Anglo-Saxon economies. Specialist mortgage banks – the savings and loans and building societies discussed in earlier chapters – have demutualized or been absorbed into larger universal banks.

Shareholder banks operate a 'transaction' banking model[5] characterized by a preference for centralized and automated credit-scoring techniques to make loan decisions, a need for high quarterly returns on equity, and a strong preference for collateral. Increasingly, the model favours the generation of profits through the securitization and selling on of loans, with the most popular type of securitized loan being RMBS. The imperatives of short-term shareholder value both incentivize excessive risk-taking and mean that lending to SMEs – involving high transaction costs for relatively small loans – does not make business sense for larger banks.[6]

By contrast, in other countries, for example Germany, Switzerland and Austria, there is a much stronger culture of 'relationship banking'. In Germany, two-thirds of bank deposits are controlled by either cooperative or public savings banks, most of which are owned by regional or local citizens or their representatives and/or businesses. These 'stakeholder banks' are more focused on business lending, do not have such stringent collateral requirements and devolve decision-making to branches.[7] They de-risk their loans not by requiring property as collateral but by building up strong and long-lasting relationships and an understanding of the businesses they lend to. Although the general pattern in advanced economies has been a shift towards mortgage lending, in Germany lending to non-financial businesses is significantly higher than mortgage lending, at 40% of GDP, whilst mortgage lending has only increased to around 30% of GDP (figure 5.2).[8] This stands in marked contrast to the advanced economy average of 70% mortgage credit and 50% non-mortgage (figure 3.1).

Empirical studies find that 'stakeholder' banks, including public savings banks and cooperative banks, maintain their lending – both mortgage and non-mortgage – in the face of financial shocks (e.g. changes in interest rates) in contrast to shareholder banks which are much more pro-cyclical.[9] This is unsurprising if their models of lending are based on relationships rather than collateral values. A bank with a long and strong relationship with a firm is

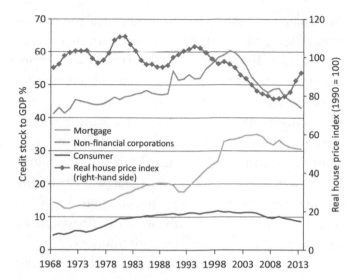

Figure 5.2. Bank credit allocation in Germany and real house prices, 1968–2013 (credit stocks to GDP)

Source: D. Bezemer, A. Samarina and L. Zhang, 'The shift in bank credit allocation: new data and new findings'. DNB Working Papers 559, Netherlands Central Bank, Research Department (2017).

much more likely to have the confidence to see it through the bad times. Evidence suggests that the general shift towards shareholder banking models and away from stakeholder banks that occurred in 2000s was a contributor to the financial crisis.[10]

State-directed finance and state investment banks
Encouraging the growth of stakeholder banks and relationship lending may take considerable time, in

particular in economies where they lack the economies of scale to compete effectively with incumbent shareholder banks. A complementary and more direct way of supporting non-collateralized lending to support productive activity, innovation and priority infrastructure (including affordable housing) would be the creation or scaling up of existing state investment banks (SIBs) (also known as 'development banks' or 'public banks'). These institutions are government-owned or -funded financial institutions concerned primarily with the provision of strategic and long-term finance to industry.[11]

Development banks are recognized as having played a crucial role in the rapid industrialization process of continental Europe in the nineteenth century, providing the patient capital necessary to build railroads and canals across the continent and in the process revolutionizing capitalist production. One of the largest examples from the nineteenth century was the French Crédit Mobilier bank, founded in 1852 by followers of the French socialist thinker and reformer Henri de Saint-Simon. Its name is revealing. In contrast to the common mortgage bank (Sociétés du Crédit Foncier) or 'land banks', which lent money on the security of *immovable* property, the Crédit Mobilier aimed to lend to the owners of *movable* property and so to promote industrial enterprise.[12] The bank funded transport infrastructure in France via low-interest long-term equity investment and bond finance, rather than the short-term higher interest lending provided by French family banks.[13] The Crédit Mobilier also enabled the development of railroads across the rest of Europe by supporting other continental development banks, via share ownership and the provision of engineers and expert knowledge.[14]

State-sponsored banks were also key to rebuilding Western and East Asian economies in the aftermath of the Great Depression and World War II, when mortgage finance dried up and property was destroyed on a major scale. The US Reconstruction Finance Corporation (RFC) was a central component of Roosevelt's New Deal, financing a huge expansion in infrastructure in the 1930s.[15] State investment banks played a key role in the rapid growth of East Asian countries in the 1970s and 1980s – the so-called 'East Asian miracle'. Globally, by the 1970s, governments owned 50% of assets of the largest banks in industrial countries and 70% of assets of the largest banks in developing countries.[16] The emergence of neo-liberal finance policies in the 1980s and 1990s, as described in chapter 3, saw a wave of privatizations of public banks. From 1987 to 2003, more than 250 banks were privatized, raising US$143 billion.[17]

State investment banks can also play an important role in stimulating innovation because of their capacity to provide patient capital to potential growth sectors that private-sector banks and investors find too risky or too low yielding.[18] For example, a recent study found that a large proportion of patient capital supporting green energy projects came from public institutions, including SIBs, rather than the private-sector sources more usually associated with financing innovation.[19] Historically and in the present, SIBs have also supported SMEs that otherwise struggle to obtain finance from the commercial banking sector and who in many cases lack property-based collateral. Both the German and Canadian SIBs, both set up in the post-war period, have played a key role in supporting SME sectors throughout their 60-year history.

After the outbreak of the global financial crisis in 2007, many SIBs across the world played a significant counter-cyclical role, increasing their loan portfolio by 36% on average between 2007 and 2009, with some increasing their loans by more than 100%.[20] As private finance has retreated from the real economy and become increasingly financialized, SIBs have increasingly stepped in to fill the gap and have become key domestic and global actors driving growth and innovation.[21]

Alternatives to bank debt financing
Bank debt has certain advantages over other forms of financing such as equity investment: most obviously it offers a return to the lender that is fixed as long as the borrower remains solvent. In contrast, equity-based investment involves the lender sharing risk with the borrower.

But since the 1980s, as banks have increasingly turned towards property-related lending, it has become less clear that bank debt provides greater economic benefits than harm. Bank credit-driven house price bubbles and the resulting financial crises have increased in frequency in recent decades, and the resulting recessions have increased in depth. Although land-backed collateral gives the appearance of security, in fact mortgages are inherently risky for banks since they are generally more illiquid, with long maturities, than banks' liabilities, which are usually deposits or short-term wholesale securities. As a result, banks have built up a major 'maturity mismatch' and are prone to increasing liquidity crises.[22] In addition, as we have seen, land's natural scarcity and fixed supply mean that land and property prices typically rise and fall more rapidly than other assets as economic conditions change. Holding large quantities of such assets arguably makes banks' balance sheets more pro-cyclical than holding a diversified portfolio of business loans.

Following the crisis of 2007–8, a number of proposals have been put forward suggesting alternatives to debt-based financing for home purchase. One argument is that mortgage debt should be more 'equity-like', with the lender sharing the risk of the home depreciating. This could involve the use of Islamic finance mortgages, where resident households and banks become the joint owners of a property until it is fully repaid by the resident. Similarly, 'shared responsibility mortgages'[23] would involve mortgage payments falling in value with the house price, but lenders would gain from any increase in the house price if the home is sold. This would protect poorer households, but whether it would be sufficient to prevent fire-sales of property in a rapid downturn, or prevent banks contributing to house price increases via excessive mortgage lending in the good times, remains to be seen.

A more permanent solution for de-linking land from finance would simply be to prohibit banks from lending against property assets. Mortgage finance under such a regime could be provided by institutional investors with long-term liabilities, such as pensions funds and insurance companies, to solve the problem of maturity mismatch. Such investors would be in a better position to agree to more equity-like repayment contracts given their long-time horizons. Banks could still play a role by issuing covered bonds backed by mortgages. Denmark has employed such a scheme very successfully for many years. Its mortgage market, despite being large relative to GDP, came out of the crisis relatively unscathed.[24]

5.3 Reforming fiscal policy: taxing land values

Reforms to the banking system would suppress perhaps the most important source of finance flowing into property – newly created credit and money. But in a post-crisis world of low interest rates, land and housing will remain a highly attractive financial asset for speculative investment. As explained in preceding chapters, domestic property has enjoyed hugely favourable taxation treatment since home ownership became the dominant form of tenure in advanced economies. Reversing this and treating landed property in the same way as any other financial asset seems essential if we are to bring house prices back to levels closer to incomes and prevent damaging rent extraction.

Economists, famously, agree on very little. But one exception is that a regular tax on the increasing value of land – a land value tax (LVT) – would be a very good idea. This was the favoured solution to the problem of land rents advocated by the classical economists and Henry George as recounted in chapter 2. Whilst there are a couple of different variants, the basic conception of an LVT would be an annual tax on the incremental increase on the unimproved market value of land that would fall upon the owner of that land.

The 'unimproved' value is important. The idea of the tax would be to capture as accurately as possible the economic gains deriving from investment in a location that are not due to the landowners' own efforts; the tax would capture for the public purse economic rent. Thus, if you put in a new kitchen on your property or converted the loft, this should make no difference to the valuation of the land underneath your property. However, if a new rail station opens near your home, giving you much faster access to the town centre, you would pay a little more tax each year because the locational value of the land on which your property stands would have increased. The converse would also apply, however: if the value of a location fell, the levy would also fall.

An LVT of this type would be both fair and economically efficient. By attaching a cost to owning land, LVT diminishes the incentive to buy land for speculative purposes – i.e. to realize capital gains – rather than productive purposes or simply to provide shelter. Knowing that any increase in the value of a property would be taxed should lead to a shift towards households purchasing a house purely on the basis of its value as a place to live – i.e. a consumption good – rather than a financial asset. There would be less incentive for developers to hoard undeveloped land. Such a tax would likely end the practice of 'land banking' or 'slow release construction' that is such a problem in countries like the UK where developers have no incentives to build and sell property efficiently because the capital gains on their assets are rising, despite the shortage of housing the country faces.

Assuming house prices would also fall as a result, other forms of more productive investment – such as investment in shares or small businesses – might become more attractive. Likewise, firms might switch more of their profits to capital investment rather than buying up real estate.

A tax on land should naturally reduce mortgage lending. Under current arrangements, as land values increase, landowners/home owners benefit from most of this increase as the value of their properties increases. In most advanced economies, they are able to capitalize this increase via home equity withdrawal. The larger the increase in land values and thus property equity, the larger the loan the bank will be prepared to make, all else being equal. Of course, the larger and longer the loan, the more of the economic rent will flow to the bank in the form of interest payments. With a sizeable LVT, most of the increase in land values flows to the public purse, leaving just a small proportion for the household to use as collateral. This would inevitably reduce the size of mortgage loans and the rentier interest profits flowing to banks.

An LVT would be also be efficient because it would not distort investment decisions in the way other taxes do. Taxes on incomes and sales taxes reduce people's spending power and thus demand in the economy. Taxes on company profits may mean firms pay lower wages or reduce investment. This is not to say all such taxes should be dropped, but rather the burden needs to be shifted towards economic rent from land. Remarkably, today 'immovable property taxes' make up just 1%

of GDP and 2.5% of total tax revenues on average across the OECD economies.[25]

Additionally, since land cannot be hidden or moved to a tax haven, land value taxation is difficult to avoid or evade – which contrasts well with many other forms of tax in a globalized world, as we have seen with recent tax avoidance scandals. Empirical studies support the theory, finding that taxes on immovable property are the least damaging to economic growth, with income and corporation taxes the most damaging.[26]

With so many clear economic advantages to LVT, the obvious question is why has it not happened already? There are major political challenges with any kind of property taxes in Western democracies where home ownership and the idea of wealth generation from the home have become culturally entrenched. There are genuine fairness issues in some cases – in particular where a household or individual is asset-rich but cash-poor, meaning a tax would significantly reduce their income.

But these concerns could be overcome. Any land tax could be introduced as part of a wider tax reform that would reduce other unpopular and regressive taxes such as income or sales taxes. Exemptions for low-income home owners, or allowing home owners to defer payment until sale, may reduce the political difficulties of land taxes. Or home owners could give up a percentage of their equity in the property each year that wasn't paid to the state, enabling the community to gain from any capital appreciation.

Another option would be to hypothecate the proceeds of a large-scale land tax evenly across the population as some kind of universal basic income, or perhaps hypothecate it to support a widely popular public service such as national healthcare. Reframing a property tax as a shared citizens' 'land dividend' could make it more appealing in the public imagination. Finally, reducing the saliency of the tax by withholding it at source from employment or pension income could make it politically more acceptable.

Ultimately, the biggest challenge facing the implementation of taxes on land may be that the most powerful groups in society tend to have the most to lose from it. Nevertheless, the stagnation of incomes and ageing demographics that have been a feature of advanced economies over recent decades suggest the policy may become more politically attractive. Recently there have been calls by major international bodies, including the OECD and the IMF, for an increase in property taxation as the tax best placed to boost growth in the post-crisis period. As incomes decline and wealth increases, and financial wealth becomes ever harder to locate and tax, it will be tempting for politicians to turn to land and property taxation to maintain tax bases.

5.4 Rethinking home ownership and tenure

The third option for breaking the housing–finance feedback cycle would be to separate the value of land from the cost of housing. By keeping land – and the economic value of land – outside the market economy and the financial system, the banking sector would be forced to find alternative ways of de-risking its lending. Few banks will be prepared to lend purely against the deteriorating value of the structures on top of a location. An effectively implemented and regularly updated LVT would go some way to achieving this goal, but the risk with any tax is that it might be phased out as the political sands shift.

Whilst the quantity of land is fixed, the rules, norms and policies relating to its usage, ownership and governance have varied immensely throughout history, and are a major determinant of the role land plays in the economy.[27] Since the enclosures began in England in the late fifteenth century, private ownership of land has risen to become the dominant form of land tenure around the world. However, as with most historical upheavals, there have been other trends running concurrently which have drawn on entirely different economic and cultural roots. Even among today's advanced economies, private landownership is not absolute, and alternative models of ownership have continued to exist.

Public ownership of land

At its simplest, public ownership serves to remove land from the market in perpetuity and to socialize rents in the process. Public landownership today is widespread and takes many forms: from public parks and public highways, to social housing and heritage buildings. Holding land under permanent public ownership can ensure that such socially desirable uses are preserved in particular locations when market forces would dictate that they make way for more profitable uses, squeezing affordability.

In Singapore, for example, a densely populated city-state island of 3.9 million residents, 90% of the land is owned by the state. Most of the land was acquired in the 1960s, 1970s and 1980s after the 1966 Land Acquisition Act that abolished *eminent domain* provisions requiring compensation to landowners. Eighty-three per cent of the population now live in housing leased to them by the government through the Housing Development Board (HDB). Land is also leased to the private sector for construction before being returned and released to residents.

The HDB also provides subsidized mortgages to HDB home owners via the 'Central Provident Fund' (CPF). This is a fully-funded, pay-as-you-go social security scheme which requires mandatory contributions by both employers and employees of a percentage of the employees' monthly contractual wage towards his/her account in the fund.[28] The CPF itself invests its balances in government debt and the government issues a variety of affordable housing loans to the HDB, creating a virtuous circle of socialized non-bank mortgage finance that has proven effective at providing affordable housing.[29] The average house price-to-income ratio in Singapore is one of the lowest in Asia and has been falling since a housing bubble in the mid-1990s. Meanwhile, the system provides the Singapore government with a handsome source of public revenues. In 2012 alone, government receipts from land sales totalled the equivalent of £9.1 billion.[30]

In South Korea, around half of all residential land development and almost all industrial land development are carried out by the Korean Land Corporation (KLC). Since being formed in 1975, the KLC has played a key role in transforming the economy by efficiently managing land and promoting economic development. The KLC's functions include developing and selling land for residential use, acquiring idle and vacant land for resale at current usage prices and developing new towns.[31] This has helped ensure that land and housing has remained affordable in South Korea.

Of course, majority state ownership of land may not be politically feasible in many Western countries. However, similar principles can apply on a smaller scale. If public-sector entities are willing and able to get hold of sufficient land for entire new settlements at current usage prices, it becomes fairly easy for the public body to capture the uplift in land values created by the development of the new town. This enables the cost of the original land purchase to be made up and exceeded, with profits put towards further upgrades to infrastructure. This is the model that was used successfully in the development of New Towns in the UK in the 1960s.

A similar approach can be used to capture the land value uplift created by the provision of infrastructure. If a public body acquires land at pre-development prices, it can then sell or lease

118

the land at development prices upon completion of the new infrastructure, thereby capturing the rent itself. This form of land value capture has been most effectively used to finance Hong Kong's Mass Transit Railway.[32]

These kinds of benefits could be achieved on a national scale by establishing national land banks or development authorities responsible for purchasing, developing and selling land for residential and commercial use following the Korean model. These land banks could use public money to buy land without planning permission and then lease or sell land to private developers at development prices following the granting of planning permission. As well as being a source of land release for housing and other development, the increase in land values could provide significant sources of revenue for the government.

Such public land banks could also potentially play a role in easing the fallout from a house price deflation by purchasing the land from property owners facing negative equity in countries with high mortgage debt-to-income levels. The land could then be leased back to them, meaning they could stay in their homes and use the additional funds to help pay back their mortgage. This would be a form of land rent socialization that, if carefully managed, could enable a gradual de-linking of finance from property.[33]

Alternative tenure patterns

Tenure patterns play an important role in mediating the impact of deregulation and innovation in the financial sector. The higher the levels of home ownership in an economy, the greater the impacts of such developments are likely to be. This is because renters are not in a position to leverage against their property. As discussed, the general pattern in advanced economies has been an increase from around 40% home ownership in the 1940s to closer to 60% by the 2000s.[34] But there are some interesting exceptions. Not all countries implemented changes in policies to boost private home ownership and mortgages. Germany, Austria and Switzerland, where home ownership rates are below 50%, provide good counter-examples.

In Germany, loan-to-value ratios at savings and mortgage banks (the main providers of home loans) were often capped at 60%. At the same time, the comparatively high levels of rent protection that were put in place in the immediate post-war years were maintained in the following decades. Leases are granted for an unlimited period of time and landlords can only evict for a handful of specific reasons, such as multiple months' unpaid rent or significant damage to the property. There are also protections against excessive rent hikes. In addition, the German tax code provides only limited incentives to take on debt. As a consequence, the home ownership rate in Germany stood at 43% in 2013 and was hence only marginally higher than the 39% ratio reached in 1950.

Switzerland is one of the few remaining advanced economies that still levies taxes on the imputed rents of house owners. It also has rent caps in many cities, and many Cantons ban foreigners from buying up property. Home ownership in Switzerland has remained around 35% in the past half century. And, also like Germany, Switzerland has a more devolved fiscal, planning and banking system, with the Cantons having considerable autonomy over these issues.

Overall, there is little evidence that economies where private home ownership dominates as a form of tenure are more productive or efficient. A number of empirical studies find a positive relationship between the growth of home ownership and increasing unemployment in a given area or country.[35] Countries with high levels of home ownership will likely have less mobile populations, reducing the efficiency of the distribution of labour and increasing the likelihood of NIMBYism (Not In My Backyard) that may impede economic development.

Easy access to housing credit may provide a short-term boost to consumption but ultimately results in greater financial fragility and growing wealth inequality. Housing policies should be tenure-neutral in terms of subsidies or taxes offered or taken by the state. The private rented sector should be made as secure as possible, with long guaranteed tenancies, limitations on rent rises and strong tenants' rights. Government should take steps to boost the stock of non-market housing, including homes with social rents, community-led schemes and co-operatives to ensure that different housing types and sizes are available in all tenures, and to make housing supply less dependent on the volatile private market in land and homes.

Finally, decent investment alternatives and secure pensions should be provided so that households are less prone to invest in the housing market to pay for their retirement, or to rely on it to fund their care in old age. When people are not fearful of never being able to get a secure, affordable home – or of missing out on a massive wealth gain – they do not feel so inclined to plough all of their earnings or borrowing capacity into housing.

6

Conclusion

Why can't you afford a home? There are simple answers to this question that have proven politically very popular: not enough homes, too many immigrants, overly zealous planning laws. Some of these issues are relevant. But there are more fundamental forces at work. The demand for landed property has become excessive and speculative. Banking systems in modern capitalist economies no longer engage in the activity our textbooks say they do. They have become primarily real estate lenders, creating credit and money that flows into an existing and fixed supply of land. This pushes up house prices, creating ever more demand for mortgage credit and higher profits for banks.

Through these profits, the banking system – and other financial institutions which buy mortgage-backed securities issued by banks – capitalizes the land rents from rising prices that their own lending helps to generate. This housing–finance feedback cycle has come to dominate late capitalist economies, squeezing consumer demand and productive investment, just as the classical economists feared when most land was used for agriculture. Yet few policy makers or economists appear to recognize this.

Land and money are two of the most neglected concepts in economic theory. Land is immobile, irreproducible and appreciates in value over time due to collective investment – none of these features apply to capital goods. Yet modern economics and national accounts treat them as one and the same. Banks create new money and credit when they lend and their lending decisions can support production and economic growth – or pump up land and house prices. A lightly regulated, profit-orientated banking system will naturally drift towards mortgage credit and away from business lending. This dynamic needs to be viewed as an iron-law, not some short-term aspect of the 'business cycle'. A 'free market' in land and credit will not optimize social welfare: it will lead to increasing economic rents, unaffordability, inequality, debt and, ultimately, financial crisis.

The difficulty is in how to intervene in a way that is politically acceptable and economically manageable. For many years the gradual expansion of mortgage credit supported increasing levels of home ownership across Western democracies, complementing rising growth and productivity. But the 1930s–1970s period was also one when mortgage credit was controlled, limited to specialist financial institutions separated from the wider financial system. At the same time, the transport revolution freed up land and enabled the creation of suburbs that brought down the cost of housing and spread wealth. Housing finance and home ownership were just one part of a broader Keynesian economic model whose primary driver was capital investment by the state, the banking system and firms.

By the 1970s, this model was under pressure. Faced with mounting public debts and difficult distributional choices, Anglo-Saxon governments liberalized mortgage finance to further spread home ownership even as growth and incomes began to falter. For a long period, rising house prices combined with liberalized finance appeared to happily be sustaining consumption and stable economic growth. Mortgage finance went global, with securitization and related financial innovations enabling mortgage debt to be packaged up and distributed across the world.

Conclusion

But this 'Great Moderation' was an illusion. The smoothing of the business cycle enabled by mortgage lending was disguising an unsustainable increase in house prices and houschold debt relative to incomes. The collapse of the sub-prime mortgage market in the US sent Western capitalism into its worst crisis since the Great Depression, so ingrained had the housing–finance feedback cycle become in our economic architecture.

'Residential capitalism' is no longer a sustainable path for modern economies. Deep systemic reforms will be required to break free of the housing–finance feedback cycle. But we are not starting from scratch. A number of economically successful advanced economies have found ways of keeping house prices at more manageable levels relative to incomes. Key to this has been maintaining tight control over mortgage credit creation. Countries with more flexible mortgage markets, high levels of securitization, variable interest rates and high levels of equity withdrawal tend to have high and more volatile house prices. The more liberalized the financial system, the stronger the feedback between house prices, consumption and the wider economy.

Complementing tighter regulations should be the creation or expansion of state investment banks and stakeholder banks able to provide long-term, high-risk capital to support innovation and provide the next generation of infrastructure needed to support the transition to a low-carbon economy. The huge demand subsidies that governments have showered on home ownership would be better employed stimulating capital investment and innovation in more productive sectors of the economy, which have suffered under austerity policies.

The public sector must also take a much more interventionist role in shaping the land market and ensuring it creates public value, not just short-term capital gains or rentier incomes for speculative domestic and international investors. Retaining public control over land and the usage of land appears key. It is remarkable that house price-to-income ratios have been moving in the opposite direction in Western democracies and mature East Asian economies such as Korea, Japan and Singapore. But in these latter economies, land and the economic rents from rising land values are socialized to a much greater extent.

If large-scale land nationalization is not politically feasible in Western democracies, then perhaps we need to accept that the dream of the 'home-owning democracy' must now be abandoned and consider the idea of more balanced tenure mixes. Western

Conclusion

European countries such as Germany, Austria and Switzerland have not experienced the rapid house price increases of the majority of the West, but all have home ownership levels at or below 50% and enjoy generous provision of rental and social housing. Anglo-Saxon economies should follow suit and end the favourable fiscal treatment of home ownership over other tenures. Private renting, public and cooperative housing systems must be properly funded. Taxation systems in general need to move away from labour and on to land rents.

And our political leaders must be brave enough to stand up to vested interests and make the case for housing returning to be primarily a source of shelter, not a financial asset. A new narrative focused on secure, affordable housing for all citizens as a right must be established, as opposed to housing as a means of securing financial wealth. As home ownership moves out of the reach of more and more young and poorer households, this process should become easier. But the key will be to find a way of de-linking our financial system and wider economy from where we live without causing financial havoc. Governments should be taking steps now to direct finance towards more productive ends, not least the creation of housing and transport infrastructure that would boost economic growth and consumption but ease pressure on our cities. A gradual, managed house price deflation is required with demand coming from investment and production, not off the back of rising asset prices. Then we can begin to break free of the housing–finance feedback cycle.

Notes

Chapter 1 Introduction

1 Demographia, *14th Annual Demographia International Housing Affordability Survey: 2018* (St Louis Metropolitan Area: Demographia, 2018), p. 10.
2 Jonathan Cribb, Andrew Hood and Jack Hoyle, 'The decline of homeownership among young adults'. Briefing note (London: Institute for Fiscal Studies, 2018).
3 US Census Bureau, 'Home ownership rates'. Federal Government (2017). Available at https://www.census.gov/housing/hvs/files/currenthvspress.pdf.
4 Angus Livingston, 'Home ownership too tough for young'. *News.com.au* (2017). Available at http://www.news.com.au/finance/economy/australian-economy/home-ownership-too-tough-for-young/news-story/eef1996640d0a9e305348dbaa864eeb5.
5 Resolution Foundation, *Home Affront: Housing across the Generations* (London: Resolution Foundation, 2017), p. 6.

6 Governing.com, 'Housing affordability for metro areas: current and historical trends' (2018). Available at http://www.governing.com/gov-data/other/rental-mortgage-affordability-for-metro-areas-historical-trend-data.html.

7 Joint Centre for Housing Studies (JCfHS), *America's Rental Housing 2017* (Harvard, MA: Joint Centre for Housing Studies, Harvard University, 2017), p. 27. Available at http://www.jchs.harvard.edu/americas-rental-housing.

8 Resolution Foundation, *The Generation of Wealth: Asset Accumulation across and within Cohorts* (London: Resolution Foundation, 2017), p. 42.

9 Joshua Robertson, '"Eye-watering prices": Australia's housing affordability crisis laid bare'. *The Guardian*, 3 May 2017. Available at http://www.theguardian.com/australia-news/2017/may/03/eye-watering-prices-australias-housing-affordability-crisis-laid-bare.

10 Òscar Jordà, Katharina Knoll, Dmitry Kuvshinov, Moritz Schularick and Alan Taylor, 'The rate of return on everything'. *VoxEU.org* (2018). Available at https://voxeu.org/article/rate-return-everything.

11 Thomas Piketty, *Capital in the Twenty-First Century* (Cambridge, MA: Harvard University Press, 2014).

Chapter 2 Land, Home Ownership and the Problem of Economic Rent

1 Katharina Knoll, Moritz Schularick and Thomas Steger, 'No price like home: global house prices,

1870–2012'. *American Economic Review* 107 (2017): 331–53.

2 See also M.A. Davis and J. Heathcote, 'The price and quantity of residential land in the United States'. *Journal of Monetary Economics* 54 (2007): 2595–620.

3 For a detailed study of the economics of land, see Josh Ryan-Collins, Toby Lloyd and Laurie Macfarlane, *Rethinking the Economics of Land and Housing* (London: Zed Books, 2017).

4 John Locke (1689), *Locke: Two Treatises of Government* (Cambridge: Cambridge University Press, 1960).

5 Adam Smith (1776), *An Inquiry into the Nature and Causes of the Wealth of Nations* (Chicago, IL: University of Chicago Press, 1976/1977).

6 Henry George (1879), *Progress and Poverty: An Inquiry into the Cause of Industrial Depressions, and of Increase of Want with Increase of Wealth; the Remedy* (London: Hogarth Press, 1953).

7 John B. Clark, 'Marshall's principles of economics'. *Political Science Quarterly* 6 (1891): 126–51, 144–5.

8 Mason Gaffney, 'Land as a distinctive factor of production'. In Nicholas Tideman (ed.) *Land and Taxation* (London: Shepheard-Walwyn, 1994), pp. 39–102.

9 OECD, 'OECD Affordable Housing Database – December 2016 indicators' (2016), Figure HM1.3.1. Available at http://www.oecd.org/social/affordable-housing-database.htm.

10 Òscar Jordà, Moritz Schularick and Alan M. Taylor, 'Macrofinancial history and the new business cycle

facts'. *NBER Macroeconomics Annual* 31 (2017): 213–63, 226.

11 Daniel K. Fetter, 'How do mortgage subsidies affect home ownership? Evidence from the mid-century GI Bills'. *American Economic Journal: Economic Policy* 5 (2013): 111–47.

12 Manuel B. Aalbers, 'The variegated financialization of housing'. *International Journal of Urban and Regional Research* 41 (2017): 542–54, 542.

13 Knoll et al., 'No price like home'.

14 Carlota Perez, 'Structural change and assimilation of new technologies in the economic and social systems'. *Futures* 15 (1983): 357–75; Richard L. Florida and Marshall Feldman, 'Housing in US Fordism'. *International Journal of Urban and Regional Research* 12 (1988): 187–210.

15 Michael Hudson, *The Bubble and Beyond: Fictitious Capital, Debt Deflation and Global Crisis* (Dresden: ISLET, 2012), p. 227.

16 John Joseph Wallis, 'A history of the property tax in America'. In Wallace E. Oates (ed.) *Property Taxation and Local Government Finance* (Cambridge, MA: Lincoln Institute of Land Policy, 2001), pp. 123–47.

17 Alvin D. Sokolow, 'The changing property tax and state-local relations'. *Publius: The Journal of Federalism* 28 (1998): 165–87, 171.

18 Glenn W. Fisher, 'Some lessons from the history of the property tax'. *Assessment* 4 (1997): 40–6, 44.

19 Michael Hudson, 'The transition from industrial capitalism to a financialized bubble economy'. Levy

Economics Institute Working Paper No. 627 (2010), p. 236.

20 Margaret Thatcher, 'Leader's speech, Blackpool 1975'. Available at http://www.britishpoliticalspeech. org/speech-archive.htm?speech=121.

21 James Meek, 'Where will we live?' *London Review of Books* 36 (2014): 7–16.

22 Aalbers, 'The variegated financialization of housing'.

23 Raquel Rolnik, 'Late neoliberalism: the financialization of homeownership and housing rights'. *International Journal of Urban and Regional Research* 37 (2013): 1058–66.

Chapter 3: The Housing–Finance Feedback Cycle and the Deregulation of Finance

1 For a full explanation, see Michael McLeay, Amar Radia and Ryland Thomas, 'Money creation in the modern economy'. *Bank of England Quarterly Bulletin* 54 (2014); or Josh Ryan-Collins, Tony Greenham, Richard Werner and Andrew Jackson, *Where Does Money Come From? A Guide to the UK Monetary and Banking System*, 2nd edn (London: New Economics Foundation, 2012).

2 Paul C. Cheshire, Max Nathan and Henry G. Overman, *Urban Economics and Urban Policy: Challenging Conventional Policy Wisdom* (Cheltenham: Edward Elgar Publishing, 2014); Nicole Gurran and Christine Whitehead, 'Planning and affordable housing in Australia and the UK: a comparative perspective'. *Housing Studies* 26 (2011): 1193–214.

3 Dan Andrews, Aida C. Sanchez and Åsa Johansson, 'Housing markets and structural policies in OECD countries'. OECD Economic Department Working Papers, No. 836 (Paris: OECD Publishing, 2011).
4 IMF, 'Chapter III. Housing finance and financial stability – back to basics?' In IMF *Global Financial Stability Report, April 2011* (Washington, DC: International Monetary Fund, 2011), p. 150.
5 Giovanni Favara and Jean Imbs, 'Credit supply and the price of housing'. *American Economic Review* 105 (2015): 958–92.
6 Òscar Jordà, Moritz Schularick and Alan M. Taylor, 'The great mortgaging: housing finance, crises and business cycles'. *Economic Policy* 31 (2016): 107–52; Dirk Bezemer, Anna Samarina and Lu Zhang, 'The shift in bank credit allocation: new data and new findings'. DNB Working Papers 559, Netherlands Central Bank, Research Department (2017).
7 Based on the average across 14 advanced economies; see Jordà et al., 'Macrofinancial history and the new business cycle facts'.
8 Bezemer et al., 'The shift in bank credit allocation'.
9 The idea that different types of credit have different macroeconomic effects was recognized by Joseph Schumpeter, and more recently in the work of economists Richard Werner and Dirk Bezemer. See Joseph Alois Schumpeter, *The Theory of Economic Development: An Inquiry into Profits, Capital, Credit, Interest, and the Business Cycle*

(New Brunswick, NJ: Transaction Books, 1983); Richard A. Werner, 'Towards a new monetary paradigm: a quantity theorem of disaggregated credit, with evidence from Japan'. *Kredit und Kapital* 30 (1997): 276–309; Dirk Bezemer, 'Schumpeter might be right again: the functional differentiation of credit'. *Journal of Evolutionary Economics* 24 (2014): 935–50.

10 Dirk Bezemer, Lu Zhang and Maria Grydaki, 'More mortgages, lower growth?' *Economic Inquiry* 54 (2016): 652–74.

11 Charles Goodhart, *Money, Information and Uncertainty*, 2nd edn (London: Macmillan, 1989), pp. 156–8.

12 Jens Lunde and Christine Whitehead, *Milestones in European Housing Finance* (London: John Wiley & Sons, 2016), p. 28.

13 Stephen A. Marglin and Juliet Schor, *The Golden Age of Capitalism* (Oxford: Clarendon Press, 1990).

14 Herman Schwartz and Leonard Seabrooke, 'Varieties of residential capitalism in the international political economy: old welfare states and the new politics of housing'. *Comparative European Politics* 6 (2008): 237–61.

15 Greta R. Krippner, *Capitalizing on Crisis* (Cambridge, MA: Harvard University Press, 2011), p. 61.

16 Greta R. Krippner, 'The financialization of the American economy'. *Socio-Economic Review* 3 (2005): 173–208.

17 Kenneth A. Snowden, 'The anatomy of a residential mortgage crisis: a look back to the 1930s'. NBER Working Paper No. 16244 (2010), p. 5.

18 Janine Aron and John Muellbauer, 'Modelling and forecasting mortgage delinquency and foreclosure in the UK'. *VoxEU.org* (2016). Available at http:// voxeu.org/article/mortgage-delinquency-and-foreclo sure-uk.

19 Avinash Persaud, 'Breaking the link between housing cycles, banking crises, and recession'. CITYPERC Working Paper Series 2016/02 (2016), p. 5.

20 Kevin Fox Gotham, 'Creating liquidity out of spatial fixity: the secondary circuit of capital and the subprime mortgage crisis'. *International Journal of Urban and Regional Research* 33 (2009): 355–71.

21 David Harvey, *The Limits to Capital* (London: Verso, 2006).

22 OECD, 'OECD Affordable Housing Database', Figure PH 2.2.1.

23 Christian A.L. Hilber and Tracy M. Turner, 'The mortgage interest deduction and its impact on home-ownership decisions'. *Review of Economics and Statistics* 96 (2014): 618–37.

24 Manos Matsaganis and Maria Flevotomou, 'The impact of mortgage interest tax relief in the Netherlands, Sweden, Finland, Italy and Greece'. EUROMOD Working Paper Series (2007).

25 Jennifer Johnson, Lorenzo Isgrò and Sylvain Bouyon, 'Milestones in EU housing and mortgage markets'. In Jens Lunde and Christine Whitehead (eds) *Milestones in European Housing Finance* (London: John Wiley & Sons, 2016), p. 415.

26 Ibid., p. 417.

27 Andrews et al., 'Housing markets and structural policies in OECD countries'.

28 Lunde and Whitehead, *Milestones in European Housing Finance*, p. 25.

29 CML, *The Outlook for Mortgage Funding Markets in the UK in 2010–2015* (London: Council of Mortgage Lenders, 2010), p. 6.

30 Alistair Milne and Justine A. Wood, 'An old fashioned banking crisis: credit growth and loan losses in the UK 1997–2012'. In J.S. Chadha, A. Chrystal, J. Pearlman, P. Smith and S. Wright (eds) *The UK Economy in the Long Expansion and its Aftermath* (Cambridge: Cambridge University Press, 2014), p. 232.

31 John Doling and Richard Ronald, 'Home ownership and asset-based welfare'. *Journal of Housing and the Built Environment* 25 (2010): 165–73.

32 Moritz Schularick and Alan M. Taylor, 'Credit booms gone bust: monetary policy, leverage cycles and financial crises, 1870–2008'. NBER Working Paper No. 15512 (2009); Dirk Bezemer and Lu Zhang, 'From boom to bust in the credit cycle: the role of mortgage credit'. Research Institute SOM Working Paper series (2014).

33 Claudio Borio, 'The financial cycle and macroeconomics: What have we learnt?' *Journal of Banking & Finance* 45 (2014): 182–98.

34 Raghuram G. Rajan, *Fault Lines: How Hidden Fractures Still Threaten the World Economy* (Princeton, NJ: Princeton University Press, 2011).

35 Charles W. Calomiris and Stephen H. Haber, *Fragile by Design: The Political Origins of Banking*

Crises and Scarce Credit (Princeton, NJ: Princeton University Press, 2014), p. 236.

36 Angus Armstrong, 'Commentary: UK housing market: problems and policies'. *National Institute Economic Review* 235 (2016): F4–F8, F5.

Chapter 4 How and Why Economic Policy Went Astray

1 Lunde and Whitehead, *Milestones in European Housing Finance*.

2 Janine Aron, John V. Duca, John Muellbauer, Keiko Murata and Anthony Murphy, 'Credit, housing, collateral and consumption: evidence from Japan, the UK and the US'. *Review of Income and Wealth* 58 (2012): 397–423.

3 Richard Barwell and Oliver Burrows, 'Growing fragilities? Balance sheets in the Great Moderation'. Bank of England, *Financial Stability Paper No. 10* (2011).

4 Hyman Minsky, *Stabilizing an Unstable Economy* (New Haven, CT: Yale University Press, 1986).

5 Dirk Bezemer, 'No one saw this coming: understanding financial crisis through accounting models'. SOM Research Reports, Vol. 09002 (Groningen: University of Groningen, SOM Research School, 2009); Steve Keen, 'Finance and economic breakdown: modeling Minsky's financial instability hypothesis'. *Journal of Post Keynesian Economics* 17 (1995): 607–35.

6 Colin Crouch, 'Privatised Keynesianism: an unacknowledged policy regime'. *The British Journal of Politics & International Relations* 11 (2009): 382–99.

7 Remarkably it was only in 2017 that advanced economies – at the behest of the EU – began separating out land values from housing assets in national accounts.

8 Charles Goodhart and Boris Hofmann, 'House prices, money, credit, and the macroeconomy'. *Oxford Review of Economic Policy* 24 (2008): 180–205, 181–2.

9 Meta Brown, Lee Donghoon, Joelle Scally, Katherine Strair and Wilbert van der Klaaw, 'The graying of American debt'. *Liberty Street Economics* (2016). Available at http://libertystreeteconomics.newyorkfed.org/2016/02/the-graying-of-american-debt.html#.V_AHIoWmqU0.

10 Sharon Parkinson, Beverley A. Searle, Susan J. Smith, Alice Stoakes and Gavin Wood, 'Mortgage equity withdrawal in Australia and Britain: towards a wealth-fare state?' *European Journal of Housing Policy* 9 (2009): 365–89.

11 Goodhart and Hofmann, 'House prices, money, credit, and the macroeconomy'.

12 Joseph Stiglitz and Alan Weiss, 'Credit rationing in markets with imperfect information'. *American Economic Review* 71 (1981): 393–410.

13 Richard A. Werner, *New Paradigm in Macroeconomics: Solving the Riddle of Japanese Macroeconomic Performance* (Basingstoke: Palgrave Macmillan, 2005), pp. 194–6.

14 John Muellbauer and Anthony Murphy, 'Housing markets and the economy: the assessment'. *Oxford Review of Economic Policy* 24 (2008): 1–33.

15 Ben S. Bernanke, Mark Gertler and Simon Gilchrist, 'The financial accelerator in a quantitative business cycle framework'. In J.B. Taylor and M. Woodford (eds) *Handbook of Macroeconomics,* Volume 1 (Amsterdam: Elsevier, 1999), pp. 1341–93.

16 Ben S. Bernanke and Mark Gertler, 'Should central banks respond to movements in asset prices?' *American Economic Review* 91 (2001): 253–7.

17 Indraneel Chakraborty, Itay Goldstein and Andrew MacKinlay, 'Housing price booms and crowding-out effects in bank lending'. *The Review of Financial Studies* (2018). https://doi.org/10.1093/rfs/hhy033.

18 Gabriele Galati and Richhild Moessner, 'Macroprudential policy – a literature review'. *Journal of Economic Surveys* 27 (2013): 846–78. Regulation had previously only focused on the stability of individual financial institutions: 'micro-prudential' policy.

19 Fredrik Andersson and Lars Jonung, 'The credit and housing boom in Sweden, 1995–2015: Forewarned is forearmed'. *VoxEU.org* (2016). Available at http://voxeu.org/article/credit-and-housing-boom-sweden-1995-2015.

20 Chris Bourke, 'The party is over for Australia's $5.6 trillion housing frenzy'. *Bloomberg.com* (2017). Available at https://www.bloomberg.com/news/artic les/2017-11-23/australia-faces-housing-hangover-tw ice-size-of-u-s-subprime-era.

21 Nathan Brooker, 'How the financial crash made our cities unaffordable'. *Financial Times*, 14 March 2018. Available at https://www.ft.com/content/ cc77babe-2213-11e8-add1-0e8958b189ea.

22 Filipa Sá, 'The effect of foreign investors on local housing markets: evidence from the UK'. *VoxEU.org* (2017). Available at http://voxeu.org/article/effect-foreign-investors-local-housing-markets-evidence-uk

23 The Economist, 'Foreign buyers push up global house prices'. *The Economist*, 11 March 2017.

24 Manuel B. Aalbers, Jannes Van Loon and Rodrigo Fernandez, 'The financialization of a social housing provider'. *International Journal of Urban and Regional Research* 41 (2017): 572–87; Caroline Dewilde, 'The financialization of housing and affordability in the private rental sector'. HOWCOME Working Paper Series (2016).

25 Thomas Wainwright and Graham Manville, 'Financialization and the third sector: innovation in social housing bond markets'. *Environment and Planning A* 49 (2017): 819–38.

26 Benjamin Braun, 'Central banking and the infrastructural power of finance: the case of ECB support for repo and securitisation markets'. *Socio-Economic Review* (2018). doi:10.1093/ser/mwy008

27 ECB/BoE, 'The impaired EU securitisation market: causes, roadblocks and how to deal with them'. European Central Bank and Bank of England (2014).

28 A. Ghent and M. Kudlyak, 'Recourse and residential mortgage default: Evidence from US states'. *Review of Financial Studies* 9 (2011): 3139–86.

29 European Commission, 'Proposal for a Regulation of the European Parliament and of the Council laying down common rules on securitisation and creating a European framework for simple, transparent

and standardised securitisation' (2015). Available at http://eur-lex.europa.eu/legal-content/EN/TXT/PDF/?uri=CELEX:52015PC0472&from=EN; Ewald Engelen and Anna Glasmacher, 'The waiting game: or, how securitization became the solution to the Eurozone's growth problem'. *Competition and Change* 22 (2018): 165–83.

30 *Ibid.*

Chapter 5: Breaking the Housing–Finance Feedback Cycle

1 Jordà et al., 'The rate of return on everything'.
2 Goodhart, *Money, Information and Uncertainty*, pp. 156–8.
3 World Bank, *The East Asian Miracle: Economic Growth and Public Policy* (Oxford: Oxford University Press, 1993).
4 Robert Wade, *Governing the Market: Economic Theory and the Role of Government in East Asian Industrialization* (Princeton, NJ: Princeton University Press, 1990); Richard A. Werner, *Princes of the Yen: Japan's Central Bankers and the Transformation of the Economy* (New York: M.E. Sharpe, 2003).
5 Michael Collins, *Money and Banking in the UK: A History* (London: Routledge, 2012).
6 Allen N. Berger and Gregory F. Udell, 'Small business credit availability and relationship lending: The importance of bank organisational structure'. *The Economic Journal* 112 (2002): F32–F53.

7 Tony Greenham and Lydia Prieg, *Stakeholder Banks: Benefits of Banking Diversity*. (London: New Economics Foundation, 2013).

8 Although it should be noted that Germany has seen the emergence of a housing credit bubble in the last few years.

9 Giovanni Ferri, Panu Kalmi and Eeva Kerola, 'Does bank ownership affect lending behavior? Evidence from the Euro area'. *Journal of Banking & Finance* 48 (2014): 194–209.

10 Giovanni Ferri and Angelo Leogrande, 'Was the crisis due to a shift from stakeholder to shareholder finance? Surveying the debate'. Euricse Working Papers, 76/15 (2015).

11 Beatriz Armendariz de Aghion, 'Development banking'. *Journal of Development Economics* 58 (1999): 83–100.

12 Michael Hudson and Dirk Bezemer, 'Incorporating the rentier sectors into a financial model'. *World Economic Review* 1 (2012): 1–12, 7.

13 Michael Hudson, 'How economic theory came to ignore the role of debt'. *Real-World Economics Review* 57 (2011): 2–24, 13–14.

14 De Aghion, 'Development banking', 85–86.

15 Walker F. Todd, 'History of and rationales for the Reconstruction Finance Corporation'. *Federal Reserve Bank of Cleveland Economic Review* 28 (1992): 22–35.

16 Eduardo Levy Yeyati, Alejandro Micco and Ugo Panizza, 'Should the government be in the banking business? The role of state-owned and development

banks'. Research Department Publications 4379, Inter-American Development Bank (2004), p. 2.

17 William L. Megginson, 'The economics of bank privatization'. *Journal of Banking & Finance* 29 (2005): 1931–80.

18 Mariana Mazzucato and Caetano C. R. Penna, 'Beyond market failures: the market creating and shaping roles of state investment banks'. Levy Economics Institute of Bard College Working Paper (2015).

19 Mariana Mazzucato and Gregor Semieniuk, 'Financing renewable energy: who is financing what and why it matters'. *Technological Forecasting and Social Change* 127 (2017): 8–22.

20 José de Luna-Martínez and Carlos Leonardo Vicente, 'Global survey of development banks'. Policy Research Working Paper, WPS5969, World Bank (2012).

21 Laurie Macfarlane and Mariana Mazzucato, 'State investment banks and patient finance: an international comparison'. Institute of Innovation and Public Purpose Working Paper 2018-01 (2018).

22 Charles Goodhart and E. Perotti, 'Maturity mismatch stretching: banking has taken a wrong turn'. CEPR Policy Insight 81 (2015); Persaud, 'Breaking the link'.

23 Atif Mian and Amir Sufi, *House of Debt: How They (and You) Caused the Great Recession, and How We Can Prevent It from Happening Again* (Chicago, IL: University of Chicago Press, 2015).

24 Jesper Berg and Christian Sinding Bentzen, 'Mirror, mirror, who is the fairest of them all? Reflections on the design of and risk distribution in the mortgage

systems of Denmark and the UK'. *National Institute Economic Review* 230 (2014): R58–R75.

25 Hansjörg Blöchliger, 'Reforming the tax on immovable property: Taking care of the unloved'. OECD Economic Department Working Papers, No. 1205 (2015), p. 6.

26 Jens Arnold, Bert Brys, Christopher Heady, Åsa Johansson, Cyrille Schwellnus and Laura Vartia, 'Tax policy for economic recovery and growth'. *The Economic Journal* 121 (2011): F59–F80; Blöchliger, 'Reforming the tax on immovable property'.

27 Andro Linklater, *Owning the Earth: The Transforming History of Land Ownership* (New York: Bloomsbury, 2013).

28 Sock-Yong Phang, 'Housing policy, wealth formation and the Singapore economy'. *Housing Studies* 16 (2001): 443–59, 446.

29 *Ibid.*, p. 449.

30 Andrew Purves, *No Debt, High Growth, Low Tax: Hong Kong's Economic Miracle Explained* (London: Shepheard-Walwyn, 2015).

31 Olga Kaganova, 'International experiences on government land development companies: what can be learned?' Working Paper, Urban Institute Centre on International Development and Governance (2011). Available at http://www.urban.org/url.cfm?renderfo rprint=1&ID=412299&buildstatic=1.

32 Purves, *No Debt, High Growth, Low Tax*.

33 Beth Stratford, 'Falling house prices could be the reboot our economy desperately needs. But only if we prepare for a soft landing'. *New Thinking for the*

British Economy (2018). Available at https://www. opendemocracy.net/neweconomics/falling-house-pr ices-reboot-economy-desperately-needs-prepare-so ft-landing/.

34 Jordà et al., 'The great mortgaging', p. 121.
35 Andrew J. Oswald, 'A conjecture on the explanation for high unemployment in the industrialized nations: part 1'. The Warwick Economics Research Paper Series (TWERPS) (Coventry: University of Warwick, 1996); David G. Blanchflower and Andrew J. Oswald, 'Does high home-ownership impair the labor market?' Cambridge, MA: National Bureau of Economic Research (2013).